LAGUNITAS BREWING
PETALUMA, CHICAGO, & THE WORLD

SO YOU WANT TO START A BREWERY?

The Lagunitas Story

TONY MAGEE

CHICAGO
REVIEW
PRESS

A Note to the Reader: This book was first published in a limited edition in 2012; it has here been revised and expanded.

ISBN 978-1-55652-562-9

Library of Congress Cataloging-in-Publication Data

Magee, Tony.
  So you want to start a brewery? : the Lagunitas story / Tony Magee.
    pages cm
  Includes index.
  Summary: "So You Want to Start a Brewery? is equal part memoir, narrative, and business story; an illuminating and hilarious account of a one-of-a-kind, made-in-America journey that culminates with the success of Lagunitas Brewing Company, one of the nation's most popular and enduring craft beer brands"— Provided by publisher.
  ISBN 978-1-55652-562-9 (paperback)
  1. Lagunitas Brewing Company. 2. Breweries—California—History. 3. Microbreweries—California—History. 4. Beer industry—California—History. I. Title.

  HD9397.U54L34 2014
  338.7'6634209794—dc23
                              2014015326

Interior design: Jonathan Hahn
Cover design: Marc Whitaker / MTWdesign.net

CONTENTS

FAUXWORD

*I*t was originally intended as a simple reconnaissance mission in the Quang Phree Highlands off the western trail, far from any sort of modern convenience. We weren't working for either side this time; we were only trying to get back something that had been lost. I was squatting with my lunch in a fecund culvert and rooting through my sad rucksack, looking frantically for a pen that I had borrowed from the now-irate old villager, whose skeletal arms held a rusty Browning Automatic Rifle two inches from my right temple.

The day smelled of oermania and the sun was a fat orange cat in heat stuck in razor wire. When I first met this old man a few days earlier, I'd noticed that he had a tremor in his sclerotic right hand, and now that tremor was far more unnerving than his temper. It was unavoidable that I'd had to borrow his pen to scrawl out a warning note to my partner in this thing, and given the circumstances at that point, my loyalty had been somewhat mis-invested. In retrospect, I had no real reason to believe that my artful partner had any inclination to live up to his end.

For a moment I forgot all about the squinty, gangrenous old man with the rifle because I was distracted by some Moroccan drumming coming from the café at the end of the block. I began to think about the Moroccan drumming, but this didn't last long, because I don't know much about Moroccan drumming. Then I thought about my missing partner and wondered if he had anything to do with the old man's quavering question to me: "Phra da manu katche gua?!" In all truth, I didn't know what to say, and not even a moment later it didn't matter, because I was suddenly lying facedown in my bowl of phra gui with little tofus of old-man brain and chunks of skull in my hair.

I heard the rifle being kicked away and up the alley as I wiped the phra gui from my one good eye and stared up at a towering figure holding a .50-caliber pistol. He was dark, lewd, sinewy, and, had I been anyone else, terrifying. This was how I first met T.M., and it is a little bit more than ordinarily grating to say that his behavior wasn't unexpected. There was an odor about him that was reminiscent of burning tractor tires, and I threw up a little bit into my mouth from it as I stood up and tried to catch my breath. He said something that sounded like, "Come with me if you want some squid." To this day I think he meant to say "want to live," but I'll never know for sure.

I raked a little more phra gui from my hair and scooped the old-man brain out of my left ear as I followed T.M. back to town. The perspective from behind him gave me a while to think about the bizarre gimp in his gait. It was a five-count gimp without the usual skitter-step on the third. I'd known men with this particular quirk before, and I had tried to avoid knowing more of them, but it was too late in this instance.

I was asked to write the foreword to this book for two reasons. The first is not repeatable here, and the second is because the first reason was so heinous. I accepted for a third, less visible reason: I had known T.M. during the earliest phases of the start of his preparatory occupation dealing in Irish slaves for the German potato plantations, which devolved into a petty smuggling operation running designer scrunchies out of Lydllandick for the gray market Eastern European hair-extension trade.

It wasn't particularly dangerous work, but it was profitable, and in the course of it all, we were introduced to more than a few attractive and cooperative septuagenarian Polish *busha*s. For my part, it was all about the money and the bushas, but for T.M., there was more to it. I'll never know for sure, but something changed in him after working closely for so long in the same circles as the notorious Doctors Putchnik and Splam and their intensive underground work around the ideas of radical fermentation and extract-recovery research.

Up to this point, I had seen things in my own life—things that keep meth-crazed housewives awake at night scratching and tearing at the skin of their pale underarm flesh, languid and bittersweet. Scenes that I would not repeat even in the darkest confessional to the most ribald Salvadorian priest. Scenarios and exchanges that are burned into my mind like gang brand tattoos and animal-cracker Velcro vest fasteners. I have heard sounds that make kittens purr and women give milk, and inhaled smells that inspire riches beyond the dreams of avarice. But I was not prepared for the visions that accompanied the fall from grace that led to the commencement of brewing on that dimly lit day in the ever-receding December 1993 in the back of the old Casa de Ricardo Building in the tortured hamlet of Forest Knolls, which borders on the equally cromulent village of Lagunitas, California, USA, NA, Earth, Sol, Local Group, Virgo Super Cluster, Space. But all of that would come later. Much later.

EMIL B. KERPUTCHINIKINIKIPURAM
N'GORNO-KARABAKH, 1979

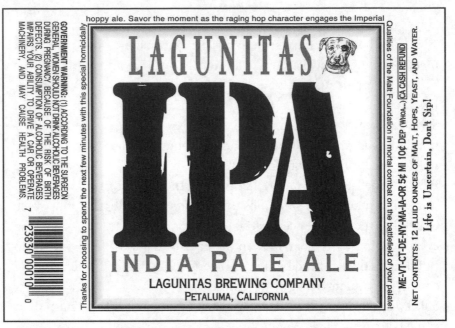

hoppy ale. Savor the moment as the raging hop character engages the Imperial

LAGUNITAS IPA

INDIA PALE ALE

LAGUNITAS BREWING COMPANY
PETALUMA, CALIFORNIA

Thanks for choosing to spend the next few minutes with this special homicidally

7 23830 00010 0

Qualities of the Malt Foundation in mortal combat on the battlefield of your palate!

ME-VT-CT-DE-NY-MA-IA-OR 5¢ MI 10¢ DEP (WHOL...) CA CASH REFUND

NET CONTENTS: 12 FLUID OUNCES OF MALT, HOPS, YEAST, AND WATER.

Life is Uncertain, Don't Sip!

First Brewed in September, 1994

"Here, have a beer. It will make you right." Ernest said to Tarzan. Tarzan had never had the true beer before and Ernest knew this would not be his last. He drank the beer quickly. It was cold, and Tarzan knew this too. He looked at the beer coolly. "Me Tarzan, you beer." Ernest looked at Tarzan and felt old. "Vas iz schviss vit da old schtuff?" Ernest and Tarzan turned to watch as Sigmund entered the room strangely. "Sigmund," Ernest said, "my old primitivo! Have a beer with us". Sigmund knew what Ernest meant and he could not bear it. They all had a beer, and it was good. Ernest said "Do you remember how it was in Stinson with the running of the dogs and how we ate crullers and got drunk on the Lagunitas Pale and stole the grunion from the young girls at the Cafe de Sand Shekel?" Sigmund thought of how Ernest could be cruel and he did not answer. He thought how only dogs were not cruel. And also how sometimes a cold beer was just a beer. Tarzan thought of nothing. They all ordered contuuzti del corratzo and spoke not of their big cigars.

Introduction

THE DAYS BEFORE THE FIRST DAYS

EVERYTHING COMES FROM SOMEWHERE

This is a memoir of starting a business. The business happens to be a brewery, which is good, because there is alcohol involved. Which can also be bad, but it makes things a lot more interesting. Ask anyone. I think it's important to point out that this is not an autobiography; it is a memoir of the business and the things that were not so visible to the public but nonetheless went on. Small brewery goings-on are the subject of a lot of very cool conversations among beer lovers, but the sausage factory behind those goings-on is another story altogether.

One can read every book ever written about "how to," but until you actually *do* it, it's all just a lot of words. Starting anything is creating, and creation is often messy. The Big Guy started the Big Business, and despite his best intentions, well, just read Genesis and it's pretty clear how unintended the consequences can be. So this is not autobiographical in that familiar way. Lagunitas is not monolithically about me; there are many others who have had huge inputs into the whole thing. But since I did start the business, and because I am the one writing this version of its story (a bonus), my preconceptions and predispositions are central to everything that occurred. Much like the Big Guy's decision with regard to the specific strength of the electrical charge of a proton, everything that can be observed now derived from early choices I made. So if you're still reading, here is how marginally I was equipped at the starting point.

My early years were flawlessly misspent: barely graduating near the very bottom of my high school class, majoring in "getting out of doing stuff," absentmindedly going to college to study product design, dropping out, then music composition, pursuing a serious buzz, writing commercial music arrangements for everything from full symphony orchestras and choruses to woodwind trios, working as a bari sax player in the marching band at a Great America theme park, joining a reggae band while perfecting that same buzz playing Bob Marley and English Beat covers on the back roads to university towns all over the Midwest, quitting the band after tripping on Mr. Natural blotter for thirty days straight (it's a long story), and finally dropping out of college with a whimper (the school told me that although I'd been there for four years, I still had three to go). I sold radio ads on the telephone, sold luggage on the street, drove a cab, did a stint as a cook, sold electronic fluorescent light ballasts, and got turned down for night watchman at a bowling alley (who knew you needed experience?). In the morning I drank MD 20/20 (Wild Plum Supreme) with a buddy while mourning the lack of opportunity in the world, investing the balance of each day at a video arcade, twenty-five cents at a time, in serial games of Defender. It was a good, long, and therapeutic fall down the stairs. Be careful if your kids claim Jack Kerouac, Quincy Jones, Wallace Stevens, and Hunter Thompson as heroes.

My other heroes were musicians and writers and one sailor: Ted Turner. That's all he was then—no CNN, no TNT or ABC. He was a transcendent sailboat-racing skipper, seemingly above the rules, and when he won he was the most quotable guy anywhere because he treated himself roughly and his success very lightly, as if he knew the bigger challenge was always around the corner. I didn't really follow sailboat racing; I followed Ted.

Somewhere deep down I always wanted to have my own business and not be employed, but that was the extent of my big picture. In any case, being a musician leads you to think for yourself, and even within a band setting, you are hired for your individuality. At one point I was actually attracted to the idea of starting a chain of dry cleaners. I think a girl I liked worked in one; I can't remember. Eventually I realized I was not going to make a living as a musician, or a dry cleaner, and over the twelve years that followed the end of those aspirations, I was fired from every job I landed. Sometimes it appeared that I quit, but I knew the difference. I guess if you say "The boss is a jerk" enough times, then you need to prove it by being the boss yourself, and then actually avoid the jerk circuit. As it turned out, it's harder than it looked, but so far, so good. Of course, I suppose you'd have to ask the guys who quit or got fired from the brewery over the years just to be sure.

Mr. Turner had a sign on his door: "Lead, follow, or get out of the way." My bosses never were willing to get far enough out of the way; you know how it is. Turner also had a knack for changing the rules when presented with a no-win scenario. A story goes that once in a race in the South Pacific he got a very bad start and decided to take a shortcut across a "natural barrier" in the racecourse—a coral reef—and won the race. He was on the sixty-one-foot sailboat *Tenacious*, which drew twelve feet of water, and he said they only hit bottom a few times. The race authorities had to make a new rule to prevent that particular innovation in the future.

Ted also liked to invest in assets, like buying prints of *The Andy Griffith Show* instead of renting them (later, he bought the whole MGM library). This is why Lagunitas never contracted out the brewing of our beer and never did that chore for others. Turner also thought strategically, four or five moves ahead, and he made things happen by acting. In the difficult craft-beer market of the mid to late 1990s, when we began, we too found our way through by thinking a decade ahead and by changing the rules as we went. It's good to have heroes whose work you'll never compare to, and in that respect, Turner is about as good as it gets.

But I have tried to lead. When I have, others have sometimes followed, and some who would not get out of the way ended up a little worse for the wear. I have had (former) beer distributors try to tell me that our success belonged to them, and there were suppliers, banks, other bad-acting bigger brewers, regulatory agencies, and municipal bureaucrats who saw our revenues as a crop to be harvested and underestimated our resolve to see change occur. It's been an interesting trip. The Pacific Northwest and Northern California markets were the most energetic craft-brewing markets in the country in 1993, and staying alive was more important than growing, but grow we did.

It is cool that Lagunitas has succeeded in helping to change some of the rules in beer and in craft brewing over the years, and in doing so we have found a clear route to our own goals, free of meaningful competition. Along the way, we cleared a path for others, who then made it even wider. It is not so well known that a lot of the things in craft brewing that are very common now are things that we at Lagunitas and a couple of other great Marin County brewers did first. Those things worked, and they caught on.

We have simultaneously built our brand into an asset that is intimately connected with our customers in markets across the country. Technically speaking, I don't think I really even understood what an asset was when I first heard other business owners use the term, but as with a lot of other fundamental concepts, I hung on to the sound of the words, figuring that one day they'd mean something to me. That might sound stupid, but when you don't even know what it is that you don't know, the best you can do is be on the lookout for clues. I have methodically worked to follow that course in a cool and genuinely American way. Four suitcases and a plane ticket to California have grown into a nice brewery and a whole life that flows from it for my wife and me, and for 500+ others. For what it's worth, my wife and I watched the 2009 stock-market meltdown as you might casually watch animals jostling in a zoo. We congratulated ourselves every morning over coffee on our wisdom of never having had any cash. We are like farmers. We have a big note to the bank, a big healthy crop still in the field, and a forecast for fair weather ahead.

A particular musician hero of mine is Frank Zappa, the ultimate individual, iconoclast, and workaholic. He spoke of something in his life/work that he called "creative continuity," meaning that every note he wrote or played, every interview he gave, every thought about future work that might occur or not, was part of a continuum; nothing could be separated out or isolated from the whole. I have long thought that others who see their life as separate from their work (work time vs. personal time) end up with only half a career and, worse, only half a life. If we were all still the hunter-gatherers (that we actually still are), the idea of "personal time" would be synonymous with starvation. The brewery is a big part of my own creative continuity. The thing about starting your own company and brand and seeing it through is that it is a long-form symphony, a composition, a thing worth doing, and you learn a lot about yourself along the way.

Socrates's challenging line "The unexamined life is not worth living" sounds like an endorsement for unrestrained personal time and reflection. But in my experience, developing a recipe and a label that you think are just super and then watching the beer sit on a store shelf unbought requires some serious reflection. Try reeling in an employee whom you like and who is important to your business—but who also thinks you're an idiot. That requires some serious reflection. Contemplation of one's navel is easy, but when you are authentically working and becoming, you really get to know yourself. You can see your true reflection in the work you do. Ask a fine furniture maker about the metaphysical and spiritual implications of cutting an imperfect full-blind mitered dovetail joint. The flaw won't be visible, but for the maker, it sorta ruins everything.

When you own a small business, you don't need psychotherapy, because all of your fears and shortcomings are handed to you every day, and if you don't face them and deal with them honestly, you and your business will fail. Craft brewing may be the most unforgiving industry of them all. From the mill to the shelf it is a crucible, and every unmanaged input and process has the potential to become a threat to the product quality, and consequentially to the business, your future, and the future of every employee who counts on you to provide the paycheck you promised. That's a heavy commitment. But it seems worth it, doesn't it?

You may—as I do—have 163 employees, but in a brewery those 163 humans are managing, or selling the product of, or balancing the ledger for maybe thirty quadrillion yeast cells on any given day. I often hear the founders of good breweries called things like "a brewing genius" or "an artist" or "a visionary" or other genuine expressions of admiration. The truth, I think, is that a guy might start a brewery for any number of reasons, but once you find yourself in the seat of power, you realize it's really a seat of responsibility, and if you are going to survive—let alone succeed—then you need to discover your inner genius, your artist, your Buddha nature, *and* your inner visionary really quickly . . . or you'll fail. John Steinbeck wrote, "Man, unlike any other thing organic or inorganic in the universe, grows beyond his work, walks up the stairs of his concepts, and emerges ahead of his accomplishments." Anyone can do it, if they recognize that they *have to. Willing* is the operative word. What are you willing to do?

Another personal axiom of mine is less poetic but every bit as useful: "You are what you did." You are not what you talk about or believe or are planning on doing more of someday. If you get hit by a falling chunk of airliner blue ice today and die, you will forever be what you actually did yesterday. *You are what you did*, so get to work.

I was born in Chicago and grew up in the vast deserts of the suburban veldt, surrounded by homes that were incubators of a next generation. Because the tract homes were almost being grown from spores and the schools were being built just about as fast, I went to a different school each year and didn't make a lot of real connections. I didn't know much, but I knew I liked the things I was learning about music. Of course, I didn't think of it this way then, but there is much that is profoundly similar between composing music and building a brand.

Musical training was actually an amazing foundation for lots of things I did later. I played and performed, arranged and wrote, ate, cut classes for, and lived and breathed music. I began playing on a tiny Magnus organ next to my bed with the names of the notes taped above the keyboard. The first thing I learned on it was the theme from *The Pink Panther*, and I played it day and night until the neighbors complained. Later I learned sax, and one afternoon in eighth grade I got

Carissa Brader, brewery production scheduler and Tony's wife

I could write my own book about living with Tony. But in a nutshell—never boring! Mostly fun. Often crazy. I've spent a lot of time trying not to think about what was actually happening and just hoping for the best—especially hard during the times when Tony was on the verge of becoming completely unglued. Which was fairly frequently, as there was plenty of crazy stuff going on. Often, in the beginning, I tried not to listen to what was happening. ("I just opened three new bank accounts so the IRS can't find us right away." Or, "We have how many liens on our house?") But Tony is the smartest and most creative person I've had the pleasure of knowing, so I figured if anyone could work things out, it was him.

I know this to be a universal truth: people love beer. I've been eternally grateful that Tony decided to make beer instead of widgets. Who wants those? But aside from the "everyone loves beer" aspect, I think there are several very good reasons why Lagunitas has been successful. The sense of fun, love, and passion that the people who work there feel flows right into the bottle. I heard someone describe Lagunitas beer as "love in a bottle." How cool is that? We've also been continuously blessed by having the most amazing people work for us and with us. Tony has incorporated some important ideas into the brand that resonate with many, many people: you're smart, you have a life, and you don't want to be preached to.

Personally, I don't really have a favorite brew. I like many of them for various reasons. But if I'm going to have more than a couple, I usually drink the pilsner.

the idea that I could arrange the music from a movie I'd seen for some friends of mine to play. The ensemble was sax, flute, oboe, and tuba. It was weird, but it was also a revelation to hear what all those black dots sounded like.

From that moment on, arranging—and, later, composing—was all I wanted to do. In high school I had one of those music teachers who gives their students the idea that everything is way easier than it looks if only you put yourself to the job. And with that, everything did become easy, at least in musical realms. I still disregarded regular classes and such, figuring that I was mastering something far more transcendent and ennobling than any calculus or film-study class could ever hope to deliver.

Later in high school I met a guy who wrote music for television commercials, and he gave me that shard of encouragement that set all sorts of other unintended and ill-advised things in motion. I was pretty darn good, but there were others who were great, and there were only about, oh, maybe two jobs available. Before I gave it up as a career, I actually scored a Pizza Hut commercial, a Bud Light ad, a Hallmark Cards spot, and a few other things. I finally caught that buzz I'd been chasing . . . and subsequently caught mononucleosis. I fell out of the scene, lived on my mom's couch for a few years, watched a lot of *All My Children* and *The Big Valley*, delivered a car to L.A. to see my dad, and, almost by accident, got a job selling printing in San Francisco in 1987.

By late 1991 I was thirty-one years old, two and a half years married, and closing on my first home. My freshly reminted self was making a surprising amount of money at the printing sales job, but it was just about to collapse. Soon my wife and I would be about $30,000 behind in federal and state income taxes. My marriage was not going so well when we bought the house with 20 percent down, drawn from income I hadn't yet paid the tax on, and when the Gulf War started, my big San Francisco bank printing customer decided not to print a planned winter Visa Card solicitation while there were US marines oozing out of the nighttime Persian Gulf and onto the beaches of Kuwait. The war quickly ended, but the bank decided to move their printing projects out of San Francisco to Seattle, thus out of my reach, and my wife and I quickly found ourselves on the brink of bankruptcy. I went from earning in the strong six figures to the feeble fives overnight, and the rebuilding took years. The repo guy called nightly about the car, the AmEx card went away, the mortgage went into default, tax collectors seized bank accounts, planned vacations evaporated, the IRS and state tax board letters appeared like new roommates, and

Tanqueray and Springbank disappeared from the cupboard while Top Ramen appeared in their place. The letters and calls deepened and "the shit piled up so fast . . . you needed wings to stay above it," as Captain Willard says in *Apocalypse Now*.

The stink of foreclosure, divorce (happily avoided!), and dissolution filled the air, and I just didn't want to become one of the bitter, foreclosed, divorced, and dissipated sixty-five-year-old printing trolls who I'd seen in the afternoon bars of San Francisco's financial district. So my scope went up to see if there was something else to do. This was the life context from which the brewery sprang: nowhere to go but up. There is a principle in chaos theory that says if a chaotic system is infused with sufficient energy, increasingly higher orders of complexity can arise. This is how the primordial ooze of the early world became Idi Amin, Richard Feynman, Britney Spears, and the Lagunitas Brewing Company. But I digress.

Visigoths, John and Lorena, or Groucho and Moe, Ales and Lagers are as different as can be. Still, we must love each for who they are, separately but equally, with liberty, and justice, for all. Cheers!

Like Adam and Eve, Isaac and Ishmael, Mao and Confusicous, Good and Evil, Day and Night, Hittites and

LAGUNITAS
PILS
CZECH STYLE PILSNER
LAGUNITAS BREWING COMPANY
PETALUMA, CALIFORNIA

Alc. by Vol. 6.2%

CA CASH REFUND

ME-VT-CT-DE-NY-MA-IA-OR 5¢ MI 10¢ DEP (WHol....)

NET CONTENTS: 12 FLUID OUNCES OF MALT, HOPS, YEAST, AND WATER.

NET CONTENTS: 12 FL. OZ. TEXAS MAKES US CALL THIS AN ALE!

Net Contents:
12 fl oz

7 23830 00012 4

First Brewed in May, 1995

In the beginning, there were ales. As far as anyone knows, the first beers made were 'top fermented', which is longhand for 'Ale'. Sometime before the 1860's, beers became popular that were made in northern Europe with a bottom fermenting yeast strain that liked the colder temperatures. Because they had to spend weeks aging before they tasted their best, they were known as 'Lager' beer. Lager is the German word for 'storage'. Since they had to sit a while, they took up more time and space and as such were harder and more expensive to make. But they were crisp and light and you could slam them down if you wanted to. Where ales are meaty, lagers are sinewy. Where ales are street, lagers are 'haute couture'. Where an ale might hit you over the head and take your wallet, lagers donate to charity and adopt stray cats. While an ale might steal your car or try to date your daughter and keep her out all night for who-knows-what purpose, a well-bred lager would offer to clean your house while you're on vacation and leave fresh scones and coffee for you when you return. Now, don't get us wrong, ales can be a lot of fun to hang out with when you're in the right mood, and if you have bail money on you. But what's wrong with livin' uptown from time to time, on a nice street, where the doormen all wear those funny uniforms, the air smells of flowers, and lagers rule the Earth.

THE FIRST DAYS

> DON'T SWEAT THE SMALL STUFF

*T*he best piece of seemingly useless advice I'd ever been given with respect to what it would take to start the brewery was this: "Imagine the largest amount of money you think it will require to get the brewery up and going, and then triple it." I can't exactly remember who said that to me, although I wish I could, because I'd like to call them and tell them that they were right. I wouldn't be calling to *thank* them, because that would be like calling to thank the guy that yelled "Stop!" right before you got creamed by a speeding bus. But right they were.

By 1992 my wife and I were slowly rising from the marital and economic ashes, a little worse for the wear and tear, while my younger brother was working for a big and famous brewpub chain in Oregon. He described the business and told me where I could get a kit to make a batch of home brew. Up until then I had never even considered the idea of making my own beer. I'd been digging getting drunk at the famous Marin Brewing Co. pub and I thought the gear for brewing was pretty sexy looking. For me, cool and functional stuff has always been sexy—like a nice reverb unit, a great speaker, or a vintage guitar—and brewing gear fit right in.

So I went down to the local home-brew supply shop my brother recommended and got the standard five-gallon plastic pail, a strainer, hop packets, yeast, malt syrup—everything you need to brew beer. I had my first brewing "stuff," and with it, I made a batch of a prefab recipe pack called "California Common Beer." It turned out pretty vile. I hardly knew why, but the instructions were simple enough, so I blamed myself and tried again. This time, I brewed a different pre-packaged recipe of a California pale ale . . . and it was transcendent. Again, I hardly knew why.

There is one basic truth to learning how to play a musical instrument: if you practice, you will get better. You may never be Itzhak Perlman (and maybe that's not really a bad thing), but you will eventually improve. I knew that the same had to be true for brewing, and so I set about discovering what it was that I didn't know.

In principle, brewing is a primitive process that Mother Nature was doing all by her omnipresent lonesome, eons before humans were imagined, with just a wad of starch, some heat, a little rain, and a random flock of yeast. Humans have evolved it into a very complex process filled with precision and control, but the essential operation is as simple as singing a major scale: *do, re, mi, fa, so, la, ti, do*. In its fullest expression, brewing approaches Stravinsky and even beyond. Learning is often less a system of affirmation than a process of elimination. As in: "I'll never let the dog lick the spoon again before I stir the pitching yeast."

As brewing awareness morphed into understanding, I developed small opinions about what I wanted to accomplish when I brewed a beer. This is another music-simile-laden moment. When you begin to really learn a melodic phrase, you ask yourself, *What do I want to try to get these notes to say?* After the first couple of brews, I remember asking the home-brew supply shop owner which yeast strain might convert the most sugars to alcohol (even then I only wanted to make stronger beers), and I remember him looking away from me and saying to the ceiling, "That is not a question a brewer would ask." I wasn't deterred, but in that moment I already knew I would be making unconventional and non–stylistically describable beers.

Up until just recently, I wrote all the recipes for the brewery myself. Now I art direct, which is just as much fun. Strict style has never really figured into our recipes. Because of that, we have never done well in the myriad brewing competitions that happen each year. "Not appropriate for style" is the most common comment. Styles are for home brewers and academics. For us, they are jumping-off points for further improvisation. As a student musician, I won plenty of medals and awards of special recognition, but in the end, that didn't mean that I would be a successful working musician. It is the work that matters. All of the awards are just fingers pointing at the moon, and you should never mistake the finger for the moon. There are maybe two judged events that we enter each year—the Great American Beer Festival (GABF), in particular—mostly because it is required in order to be part of the public tasting sessions that follow them.

But even if we *were* to accidentally win a medal at GABF, I wouldn't make a big deal out of it with posters or advertisements. Some beer companies will, and that's cool for them, but it's not important for us. I mean, if you win, it doesn't mean that you will succeed, and if you lose, it doesn't mean you will fail. So why not just avoid the background noise altogether and get back to work? But I digress.

Back in early 1993 I was reminded of something called the Florence Nightingale effect, where wounded soldiers routinely fall in love with their nurses during recovery. I think that brewing was like my nurse as I came out of an unusually hard period in my life, and by the third batch (after three weeks of brewing), I was already sitting on the living room floor making up a pretend income statement and intensely adding up columns of guesstimated production volumes and costs and overhead and everything I could think of to get some idea of how much beer I would have to make to break even. My wife and I were $38,000 behind on taxes by then, and at that point I aspired merely to break even. But before I had any idea what I was going to do or what it was going to take to get 'er done, I rented a space in a nearby building, applied for a license, bought and installed a three-tier home-brewing setup, and began plans to install a real commercial brewery . . . while also still learning how to make beer. By December of that same year, all of these things actually happened.

My crude initial income statement predicted some break-even sales levels that were, well, wrong. These were the first of more than a dozen annual projections that I worked hard to perfect, and I was never even close. Over time we got better at knowing why the projections were so wrong, and I felt good about that . . . sorta.

I didn't want to have a retail brewpub. Personally, I was in a deep bunker mentality following all the home and economic problems I'd experienced, most of which persisted. I was still a full year behind on all of our personal taxes. The thought of having to be Mr. Hospitality and host customers was a nonstarter. I would do it the way another great San Francisco brewery (Anchor Brewing) did it: with wholesale trade. The margins would be thin, but I would do all the work myself, and whatever crumbs were left over, I'd feast on them. I was not in a position to borrow; there was no home equity to tap, no savings, no rich relations. So I would take the money from our household income. But when I began looking for equipment, it seemed to be everywhere, and all of it was too expensive.

By 1993 the craft brewing industry was in the middle of a big burst of growth, which would eventually lead to the 1995 opening of one thousand new breweries . . . and the later mess of closures. But that was a few years out, and as it is in any gold rush, the folks making money were the ones selling shovels and pancakes. Fourteen-barrel brew houses could cost upward of $100 million, and that was just one of many necessary components. I happened on a small classified ad in the back of the *New Brewer* magazine, and in short order I was talking with the ebullient John Cross. He not only wanted to tell me about equipment, but he wanted to discuss everything about the brewing process, including mash and fermentation temperatures. I really needed a guide to the gear and the process. I'd only brewed ten or twelve batches by that time and mostly knew only what I'd read. Noonan, Owens, Papazian, McCabe, and Burch were my constant reading companions. So after talking to John Cross, I drove to the tiny southern San Joaquin Valley mountain town of Springville to visit his shop and see what accidental opportunity might exist. Pay dirt was waiting.

John Cross was the guy who imported most of the thousands and thousands of 210-gallon European beer serving tanks they call Grundy Tanks. A little background: in much of Europe, breweries once outfitted pubs with 210-gallon stainless bulk-tanks instead of the 15.5-gallon kegs we use here in America. European brewers would send out tanker trucks full of beer to fill up these storage tanks at the pubs, sorta like a gas station. I guess it all worked out well for a while, and was certainly more efficient than transporting the long pipeline of expensive kegs that we use here in the States, but in the end, the beer suffered. I'm sure there were problems with sanitation and oxygen pickup, but John Cross told me that the biggest problem was that the "publicans" learned that they could remove the top of the tanks with the right tool, and from there it was a simple matter to top a tank off from time to time with a little tap water.

What was good for the publican wasn't good for the brewers, and at some point the brewers uniformly cut off the bulk deliveries and switched to fifty-liter kegs. That put thousands of used Grundy Tanks on the market, so John Cross and a couple of others bought them up, cheap. They brought them across the pond and got out their TIG welders. The versatile tanks were used in many different capacities, and they provided the raw material for hundreds and hundreds of US microbreweries. The tanks have been used and modified to serve as kettles, mash tuns, fermenters, serving and bottling tanks, glycol tanks, CIP tanks, dry-hop dosing vessels, yeast brinks, you name it. I've used and modified seven of them myself, including using one as the boiler for a still. There is one now serving as decoration in our Beer Sanctuary, and another has a continuing career as a fermentation blow-off foam receiver in our brewery. But back to John Cross . . .

After seeing his standard "works-in-process" three-vessel systems, I was starting to get discouraged by the true cost of my fantasy, and I said so. John grew quiet for a moment and then shot me a sideways glance and rubbed his chin. He had a cool dog, and it grew silent and laid down. The wind stopped and a cloud passed in front of the sun. This is the truth, and there have been a dozen moments like this in the course of events at the brewery.

John looked at me in silence, sizing me up for the opportunity he was thinking of presenting, and then he spoke. He told me he had a one-off brew house he'd built for delivery to Russia, where he was building brewery systems into forty-foot shipping containers for a plug-and-play sort of installation. This one had been cancelled and was incomplete. But he'd already been paid for the parts to build it. He took me into the back shed, where it sat. It was a twenty-five-foot-long rectangular stainless-steel box with a hot-water tank, a mash tun, a two-hundred-gallon kettle, and all the pumps and piping built in. It took three hundred amps of electricity. (Seems there isn't much natural gas available in rural Russia.)

I didn't have any idea what I was looking at from a technical standpoint, but I figured that John knew more about brewing and brewing equipment than I did, so I blinked and asked him how much he would want in order to complete it for me. He was quiet for a long time, and I figured he was rethinking the whole deal. But then he looked up at me and said the unthinkable: $5,000. A few weeks later, I excitedly told Brendan Moylan of Marin Brewing Co. that I was building a brewery and that I'd bought a brew house for $5,000. He looked at me blankly and asked if it was made of stainless steel.

In theory it was impossible, but I saw that I could get a real brewery going for about $30,000 in gear and rent, which seemed doable. I was by that point about $42,000 behind in my income taxes, and the revenuers of the world were no less impatient than they were before, but I figured that if I were going to be a slave, I would at least choose my own work. I wanted out of printing very badly. Although I'd found a little new business to replace what I'd lost, I could see that the boom-and-bust cycle of printing would be eternal. This was (and still is) why all those old-pro printing guys were getting loaded every afternoon in the bars of downtown San Francisco. No, I would pay Uncle Sam and his cousin Governor Pete Wilson soon enough, but first I'd change careers.

I didn't really ask my spouse if this was a good idea or not; I knew what the answer would be. I read one time how the entrepreneurial urge is, in it purest incarnation, a sort of seizure—nearly involuntary, like speaking in tongues or getting married in Vegas. It was like that for me, and this was the moment where reality and finance parted ways.

Later I was talking with an erstwhile and well-known equipment supplier about an overpriced little keg machine, and he told me that if I was going to be in the wholesale brewing biz, then my kettle needed to be at least thirty barrels or I was doomed. A little later I bought a small keg machine for $5,000 and was subsequently told by a famous brewing educator that I should have spent at least $15,000, and that if I didn't do so I was "doomed to failure, and this industry does not need any more failures." Word. In any case, the more I was told that it would never work, the more determined I became. Sort of like the drunk hotel partygoer who climbs out onto the fourth-floor balcony, determined to jump into the pool, while everybody yells, "You'll never make it!"

I would eventually find out that all the naysayers were correct. But by using the shoestring at hand, I cobbled together a brewery that could produce about one thousand barrels per year with two John Cross–built Grundy Tanks as fermenters, and the weird little electric Russian brew house. At the time, I was only planning to produce unfiltered draft beer and to market it as a private-label product to twenty or so bars and restaurants in San Francisco and tourism-heavy West Marin County, where I lived. I would brew, filter, keg, sell, deliver, and service it all solo, while still maintaining the nice chunk of printing work that I had rebuilt. If worst came to worst, I could even live in the 750-square-foot brewery space. Eventually those worries ended, but it took a while.

Six months into the business, the summer of 1994 had gotten very busy. I'd already bought one additional fermentation tank and needed a fourth one to keep up. My days went something like this: I would mill grain around 9:00 PM the night before a brew, wake up at 3:00 AM, mash in at 3:30, knock out the kettle at 7:30, clean up by 10:00, and then do printing work all day—sometimes even while I'd be making keg deliveries—after which I'd often have to fly to L.A. overnight to meet my printing customers at the plants to approve press runs, while still doing the brewery business from there too.

At some point in June 1994 it all got to be too much, and while the little brewery was just beginning to carry its own weight financially by selling only the private-label draft beer, I needed to hire some help. This single decision to increase the brewery's daily cash "burn rate"—and the resultant need for increased sales volume to support the first payroll position—was the beginning of many crazy years of what I can only describe as being chased down the street by a pack of wild dogs.

When I began, I thought that the brewery would be like a custom cabinet shop. I'd do everything, and I'd keep all the winnings, however meager. But this was unrealistic. Adding that first employee was like the first punch thrown in a crowd. The consequences were complicated, like trying to describe what happens while falling down a flight of stairs. It went something like this; try to hang with me . . .

There is too much work and too many good customers for you to do a good job all by yourself. You go from being an A student in five things to being a C+ student in thirty things. So you hire one new guy, and consequently your daily cost of operation goes up. Then you need to sell more beer to pay for the change, which you can, so you do. To make the extra-tasty brew you need to buy more ingredients, which you can, so you do. But unless you sell the beer COD, you will probably need to pay for the ingredients before you get to collect for the beer the ingredients will become, which means you need a little more cash up front.

It's all about the "time of arrival" of the money to your checking account. Your little brewery is a little bit profitable, but you are growing quickly, and the "time of arrival" thing is getting tighter and tighter, because you seem to need more than the little bit of money that you are generating in profits if you are going to pay your bills on time. Checks are clearing your account faster and faster. Since you have another day job, you just put your paychecks from that directly in the brewery because things seem to be going so well, and you feel confident.

So you grow quickly, you pay for more materials and then an employee salary, but you have to do all that before you actually collect for the brew you're delivering, and while you *are* technically profitable, cash somehow remains scarce. Suddenly you realize that you need another fermenter and a few more kegs, because you are growing and you are starting to short orders, so you buy another fermenter, which also takes more money than you are making. Maybe you have a bank that will lend you money, but in 1996 I didn't, and if you're small, you won't either. I had to land more printing jobs instead.

Every month now you are brewing and selling a whole lot more than you did the previous month, and you have a hard time keeping up with the hand deliveries to your expanding new customers. You need a distributor to better handle the deliveries so you don't lose those customers over service problems. The distributor needs to make money on the kegs, and you can't easily charge a lot more for them, so you reduce your selling price to the distributor. Now you really need to make and sell more beer to get that little bit of profitability back up, but your brewer is getting worn out by the long hours, so he wants a raise, and you have to hire him an assistant. Now you need to sell even more beer to pay for the new guy because your sales are increasing and you are buying more ingredients. And you are now waiting to get paid from the distributor—and since you only have one distributor, and it is going well, you decide to get more—and then you need a salesman, and then another distributor, and another salesman, and then you need more brewers, more ingredients so you can make more beer, so you can sell more beer, so you get more distributors. One day you realize that you need a bookkeeper. The good news is that you have a growing business and brand and you feel like you are making beers that haven't been made before (and *that* is exciting!). Now you feel great, so you buy even more fermenters and kegs, and you hire more salesmen, and this takes even more money. The good news is that you'll never have to pay to get drunk ever again!

There is this invisible and prickly detail that takes a while to get your mind around, or at least it took me a while: the mysterious financial bugaboo called the cash-flow statement. The cash-flow statement is the first derivative of the income statement and balance sheet. It all comes down to sources and uses of cash. The uses are inventory and receivables. They are serious liquidity sponges—meaning that they soak up cash. If you don't have or can't generate that cash, then you will pay your bills slower. Suppliers understand this better than you do, so they watch for it and pull the reins tight to prevent you from getting too upside down with them. Their basic response is to require you to pay for supplies COD, which empties your bank account pretty quickly.

One of the interesting things about starting something when you don't know what you are doing is that you are constantly presented with very specific details that you have to master, or you will be consumed by them. They are things you'd never heard of before that must quickly become second nature. Things like heat-exchange ratios, hemocytometers, commercial lease negotiations, basic fluid dynamics, workman's compensation insurance, trucking companies, payroll taxes, and cash-flow statements. I don't know about anybody else, but the learning curve was simultaneously the most energizing and the most exhausting part of growing Lagunitas. I can remember the gears beginning to grind while trying to grasp something complex and unfamiliar at 3:45 on a Friday afternoon, while the uptake of glucose in my brain emptied the last of its meager reserves.

Where was I? Oh yeah . . .

The two things that will most reliably devour all of your cash are inventory and receivables. Everyone has heard these words, and in the past when I'd heard them discussed, I just narrowed my eyes and nodded my head thoughtfully, murmuring, "Mmmm, uh-huh, I see." But suddenly these tiny words were threatening to ruin Lagunitas. Inventory and receivables are the raw materials in waiting, product in process, finished product on hand, and the money you are waiting thirty days to receive for product you've already sold.

Stay with me now (I can already hear you murmuring, "Mmmm, uh-huh, I see"). If you buy malt and hops on, say, May 1, and by May 15 you have a great beer that you package and sell by May 20, you hope to get paid for it around June 20, *if* your distributors mail their payments on time. Meanwhile, the malt and hops bills are due promptly thirty days after you bought them—in this case on June 1! Along with all of your other expenses (like payroll and rent and pump seals), you also need to pay your malt and hops bill nineteen days before you have any hope of seeing the money for the great beer you made from them.

Say you sell $20,000 in beer one month, but you are growing fast, so the next month you sell $30,000, and your cost of goods sold (which means all the costs of making this great beer) is 65 percent of your selling price (which it might well be when you are small). That means that you need to find $7,000 to cover the increased raw-material bills for those painful nineteen days, because you need to pay your bills on time. But since you're still a very small brewer, you are only barely profitable, so maybe you made 10 percent (*maybe*), or $3,000, so you are conclusively $4,000 short for the month (the difference between your cost of brewing and your profits).

People like your beer and you are profitable, but you are running out of cash. It's creepy. Imagine this going on month after month after month, year after year. You are happy because you are growing and the scene is totally cool and you are having fun doing it, but you are becoming skinnier and more anemic every month. Like a high school kid in a growth spurt, no matter how much you eat, you can't put on a single pound. Now the thing that happens while you are busy running your brewery is that you start to pay your bills later and later, and this gets on your suppliers' nerves quickly. The big companies who are selling you these raw materials already know about this scenario, and they can get pretty impatient with your exciting learning process.

NET CONTENTS: 1 PINT 6 FLUID OZ

7 23830 00003 2

LIMITED RELEASE

LAGUNITAS

CappuccinO
STOUT

ALE BREWED WITH COFFEE

Brewed with
Sebastopol's Own
Hard Core Coffee

I.B.U. 29.50
O.G. 1.076

ALC. 8.4%
BY VOL.

The Lagunitas Brewing Co. Petaluma, Calif.

ME-VT-CT-DE-NY-MA-IA-OR 5¢ MI 10¢ DEP (WHOL...) CA CASH REFUND

Coffee is my shepherd; I shall not doze. It maketh me to wake in green pastures, It leadeth me beyond the sleeping masses. It restoreth my brain, It leadeth me in the paths of consciousness for it's name's sake. Yea, though I walk through the valley of the shadow of sleep. I will fear no artificial sweetener for thou art with me; Thy cream and thy sugar they comfort me. Thou preparest a carafe before me in the presence of my zzz's, Thou anointest my day with sunlight; My cup runneth over. Surely richness and flavor shall follow me all the days of my life: and I will dwell in the house of Cappuccino forever... Let us sip... or whatever... 1.707.769.4495

First Brewed in January, 1994

*C*offee is my shepherd; I shall not doze. It maketh me to wake in green pastures. It leadeth me beyond the sleeping masses. It restoreth my brain, It leadeth in the paths of consciousness for it's name sake. Yea, though I walk through the valley of the shadow of seep, I shall fear no artificial sweetener for thou art with me; thy cream and thy sugar they comfort me. Thou preparest a carafe for me inthe presence of my zzz's, Thou anointest my day with sunlight; My cup runneth over. Surely richness and flavor shall follow me all the days of my life; and I will dwell in the house of Cappusccino forever... Let us sip... or, whatever...

THE TYRANNY OF FAST GROWTH

*T*his is the tyranny of fast growth that no one outside the business ever really sees. If you are an employee, the good boss will make sure that the one bill that always clears the bank is payroll, so you keep coming in to work to keep the thing going so that the business has at least some chance of catching up someday. And to make the whole thing tougher for the boss, most people inside the business don't ever see the stretching that is occurring, and if they work in the plant brewing or bottling, all they see clearly is a lot more beer going out the door, a lot of new money being borrowed for equipment, and not much more in their pockets for the effort they are expending, which is considerable.

Ask your favorite local brewery owners how many of their early brewers and employees are still with them. The answer will almost uniformly be zero. For me this has been a source of great anguish, because the problem is subtle, and explaining it sounds like hocus-pocus accounting stuff that doesn't really exist, although everyone is certain it does. For the owner it is heartbreaking when the people who have helped make the first part happen leave before the promised land appears on the horizon. Kinda makes you seem like one of the jerks you worked for in your previous life. I guess it is part of what my folks meant when they said, "You'll understand when you grow up." This basic cash-flow business scenario ought to be taught early in every classroom so that we can all be on the same page when things get hard. It was certainly all news to me, given my vast inexperience, but I was surprised to find out that even some smart kids from a nearby hard-to-get-into, very expensive, and world-class business school, who once came to do a study project on the brewery, had only the vaguest of notions about the sources and (most important) uses of cash in a small and fast-growing business.

To be honest, when I asked them what a brewer should do in this ubiquitous situation, one of the MBA students answered, "Well, you need to raise more capital." This is the basic truth, but capital—specifically equity capital—is the most expensive financing you'll ever take, if you can even find it. The grad student meant that I should sell stock, and he was correct, but that share that you might sell on that one day for $50 will be worth $5,000 someday if you succeed. That means the $50 will eventually cost you $4,950!

I didn't have any deep pockets nearby, my own had quickly emptied, and I didn't want to sell any more shares of my little company than I absolutely had to. Eventually, when I had to move the brewery into a larger space, buy bigger brewing stuff, and do a bunch of building renovations, I needed to raise money. I got it from some old friends and from some new friends, and in 1998 I traded about half ownership of the brewery for $650,000. At the time I couldn't borrow it from anywhere, so I had to raise it by selling stock. It seemed like a lot of money in 1998, but later, in 2011, I easily borrowed more than $9 million from a local bank with just a couple months of phone conversations and some routine paperwork. We even had two other banks competing to lend it to us at the same time. Jeez . . . snotty-nosed MBA kids.

Back to the cash nightmare. A few years down the road, you've grown your little brewery quite a bit. You've found ways to cover the cash deficit (more on how to do that and how *not* to do that later). Now imagine that you are selling $1 million worth of beer every month; you have better margins, and your cost of goods sold is more like 50 percent. That means that if you grow at 30 percent, you'll sell $1.3 million the next month (yahoo!) and you might need something around $150,000 to fund just those pesky inventory and receivable costs. Well, if you are good enough to operate at a 12 percent net profit and you made $156,000, then from a cash standpoint, after you cover your cost of goods sold, you might get to keep about $6,000 (about half a percent!) with which to pay all the other new hires and buy all those tanks and kegs and fuses and pump seals. It's better, but the tanks and kegs you'll need will cost way more than the $6,000 in cash you might have kept. Sheesh. Breathe, borrow, breathe, borrow, breathe.

This is one reason that you see so many breweries now making very strong beers that sell for more money per ounce: the perceived value is greater, and so they can charge more. The higher your revenue per barrel, the easier all the trouble can be to manage. In 1995 we were making stronger beers like we still do today—because I like them—but it would have been hard to charge today's higher prices and still grow nicely. This was because craft beer was still relatively new, and stronger beers were not really in demand yet. San Francisco was a pretty developed craft-beer market at the time, yet most bar owners refused to carry any of our seasonal brews (which were all much higher than 7.5 percent) because they felt that they would sell fewer pints and have bigger problems with drunks. Most of the breweries that now brew stronger and more expensive beers developed in markets that didn't like craft beer in 1995, and so when their markets "woke up," craft beer as a whole was further evolved, and those brewers enjoyed early state market rules that were more receptive to higher strength and more expensive brews.

But at the time of our entry into the San Francisco beer scene, every brewery in the country seemed to be trying to sell and deeply discount their beer there, including many larger craft breweries that are long gone as a result. The Bay Area was, in the early 1990s, a focal point for growth for most of the breweries that originated in the Pacific Northwest, as well as being the all-important home market for the handful of California-born brewers. For the Pacific Northwest brewers, the Bay Area represented a huge population base a good six hundred miles from home. That distance from their homies allowed them to be very aggressive in their marketing and to deeply discount their beer without feeling like they were harming their brand's image. Back then, being a national brand wasn't so realistic, so California seemed a long way away—a safe distance. Craft beer was pretty cheap in those days, and we had to ante up!

When I look at reviews on beer rating sites, I sometimes read comments about our beers that say things like, "A nice beer, but for a few dollars more there are other beers that have bigger flavors." There is a chicken-and-egg thing at work here: making the beer stronger does not really cost the brewer a few dollars more, but making stronger beer allows the brewer to *charge* a few dollars more. We make our beer with the flavors that we do—and sometimes they are more delicate—because we like them that way, not because we are saving on ingredients to keep them cheap. It is interesting how different perception is from reality in this way, and I often wonder how it will all turn out down the road.

Uh, but I have indeed digressed.

So let's return to late 1994, when, after only nine months in our little brewing home in West Marin's tiny hamlet of Forest Knolls, I got a call from our septic tank. In putrid tones, it told me we had to leave, and quickly. The septic tank also called the neighbors. It called the busy street out in front of the brewery, the playground behind us, and then it called the county.

It was the end of innocence for the brewery, and leave we did, quickly landing a lease in nearby Petaluma. I'd sunk a large fistful of piastres into getting that first little plant running, and losing that investment was a drag, but the new situation was so much better. The move and the new space were both expensive, and so (by now you know what's coming) we would have to sell more beer. But the bigger problem was that my little seven-barrel electric Russian brew house was quickly running out of juice, and after the move I would have no money left for a new one, let alone a larger one. So I called up the honorable Mr. John Cross again, and in the single most amazing act of generosity ever, topping his first act of Russian brew-house generosity,

Ron Lindenbusch, first marketing guy and current chief marketing officer (CMO)

Tony was like the mad scientist that had just discovered the secret formula, but the recipe wasn't a brew, it was a way of being. He was selling kegs out of the back of his Ford Ranger; I had never seen anything quite like it. When I first hitched up to the brewery, I just hoped that the horse could go a long way on very little water . . . maybe it could live on beer! For me, [working at Lagunitas] has paid off in ways far greater than money. It's like being part of a big family where everyone is allowed to be who they are, as long as they bring something tasty to the potluck dinner. I never thought that I would be part of something this cool for this long . . . I always thought that I was relatively unemployable! The experience has been like a roller coaster ride where all the hills are going down and you're going as fast as you can go and you can't help but wonder if the damn thing can possibly stay on the tracks . . . we've only lost a few of our riders so far. Ever since that first batch rolled off the bottling line in '95, our IPA has been my favorite. It has a flavor that I just can't get tired of . . . no matter how hard I try!

he offered to build a bigger one for me. He asked only that I make a monthly interest payment on the cost of building it. Once I was resuscitated, I accepted. That money was later repaid in full, but never the debt.

During this time, we were cutting off the tops of our existing fermenters and welding in additional sidewalls to make them taller and increase the capacity. A friend of the brewery stepped in and lent me the money to do this work interest-free, with only my promise of later equity when we issued stock. These sorts of things occurred far more frequently than the Monte Carlo method would suggest was possible. It is good to have friends.

By 1995 things were still financially very uncomfortable, and I desperately needed to get more money into the business. Up in

Petaluma, we were still only packaging beer in kegs, which don't really bring in much profit. Back then, a brewery might have sold a keg to a distributor for about sixty-five dollars wholesale. So a fourteen-barrel batch would bring in around $1,820. The same fourteen barrels converted into bottled beer, however, might bring something like $2,960 wholesale. I might be financially as dumb as a bag of hammers, but I reasoned that if there was more money in play, I might have more flexibility. I knew that bottled beer has a lot more ingredients: in addition to the actual beer, there's glass, labels, crowns, carriers, and cartons. So the pesky inventory-and-receivables thing would be harder, but I plunged in anyway.

I had a lot of decisions to make about the new bottled brand, but oddly enough, the heaviest one was what we would charge for it. It was a very turbulent market when we were ready to go. I looked at some market info (IRI) reports and saw that the average selling price of almost every six-pack brand in the top twenty was $5.99—and some even less. This seemed really, really cheap, but it was the world we were in. The Pacific Northwest brewers were literally dumping their excess capacity into the San Francisco market. They all had frontline six-pack prices of $6.99, but they did every-other-month promotional prices of $4.99, and so the average fell in the middle. I wanted to make sure that, at every opportunity, I would aim Lagunitas at participating in the market with only the best brands. That didn't mean other craft brewers. At that time, it meant imports.

I had read an interview with Fritz Maytag where he described his reasons for thinking that he could succeed at Anchor Brewing from his very earliest days at the brewery. He said how there was increasing growth in consumer interest in the more flavorful imported beers at the time, and he figured that if he could make a beer just as good, then he could deliver it fresher, and it would have the bonus of being locally produced. Imported beers were more expensive, and so he looked to their pricing as a model. For my part, I felt strongly that markets and conventional wisdom change way faster than people do, and that if his observation was true in the early 1970s, then it would probably still hold true. Besides that, craft beers made up something like 2 percent of all beer sold, and imports were 12 percent, so it was a far more target-rich environment.

In any case, when a beer lover walked into the beer aisle in those days, and he had six dollars to spend on a six-pack, there was a two-to-twelve chance that he would grab a microbrew and a ten-to-twelve chance that he would grab an import. I liked the import odds a lot better, so I needed to price similarly and participate in the market similarly. These were huge breweries, but I wanted them to be my peers. We weren't sophisticated enough to do effective promotional pricing yet, but I felt that if we wanted to play with the big boys, we'd have to ante up. So we set our everyday price at $5.99 for a six-pack. That took courage, but I thought it was important to present our beer alongside the very best, and I wasn't interested in taking part in the crazy discounting measures the other craft brewers were using.

In the end, many of the good craft brewers that I was trying to keep pace with screwed the proverbial pooch by engaging in that suicidal discount pricing. It cost some of them their businesses and others their brand equity, because nobody was ever willing to pay full price for those beers after that. The toll was huge. The crummiest part was that most of those brewers were from the Pacific Northwest and, as I mentioned, in their home markets they never would have taken part in that kind of discounting. They all became hooked on the volume that the comparatively populous California market could deliver. Plus, they didn't have to care about the market as much as us because they didn't live here. It made for a difficult market entry for us, but it also made us tough. We offered our beer at a competitive price, but because we offered our beer at that one price *all the time*, it seemed like a fair deal to people. There was no *if I wait a month, it'll be cheaper* thinking going on with Lagunitas beers, so we created a nice and authentic image of value.

LAGUNITAS

Peach Wheat ALE

Life's a Peach!

Brewed and Bottled by the Lagunitas Brewing Co.
Petaluma, California

O.G. 1.058

I.B.U. 16.8

First Brewed in August, 1994

*I*n certain parts of the world, they make ales which are fermented with rowdy, un-civilized, wild, and thoroughly un-cultured Yeasts that produce bone dry, sour, face-puckeringly tart beers called Lambic Ales. The only thing to do is throw in whatever sweet stuff is around: Pears, Apricots, Cherries, Peaches, Avacados, Berries, Leeks, Bok-Choy, Radiccio... whatever. Well, our ale didn't start out face-puckering, but we threw the Peaches in just the same. This is number two in our Single-Batch Series. We liked it, and hope you do too. Give us a call sometime and come visit the Brewery in Petaluma at 1322 Ross Street. Cheers!

BUT WHAT KIND OF BEER...?

> **BUILDING A BEER IN MAKE-OR-BREAK TIMES**

*W*e entered the world of six-pack bottled beer with a pale ale and an amber ale. The pale was our most popular.

Sierra Nevada Brewing Co. was then, as it is now, the second-largest craft brewer in the country, and it is just right down the proverbial street from us. They were solid in their approach to the world, and because of that, people loved them. People respected them. People bought the beer. As time went by, I realized that it was bad form for us to pretend we could crowd out this other brewer of a great pale ale, and it was just pissing into the wind, because we would never get any draft business going. Bar owners saw no reason to have two pale ales, because they wanted variety for their customers. If I was going to get any Lagunitas draft business with our pale ale, I would have to fight with Sierra Nevada, and even if it was possible to do (which it probably wasn't), you don't do that to a company you respect. In any case, I only wanted to compete with imported beers and never with other craft brewers. That is still true today. I can brag, though, that for several years we had the second-best-selling pale ale in California, after Sierra Nevada's! A very, very, very distant second, but still . . .

I needed to find a way to sell around Sierra Nevada and to coexist without our two companies bumping into each other. When we brewed our first fourteen-barrel batch of our IPA as a one-hundredth-brew celebration, complete with our new yeast, in 1995, the beer came out so flawlessly that I instantly saw our way through to daylight. We would be *the only brewery in California* to lead with an IPA (which is way different from today). An IPA wasn't better than a pale ale, but it was a premium version of a pale ale. That would be our point of difference.

Quickly, I also realized it was likely that down the road the IPA category might well be *the* category because it is just such a flavorful beer, and it answers most of the things people like about pale ales in the first place. In many ways I wish I hadn't been quite so right about that hunch. IPAs have now become a seriously crowded flavor area, but ours continues doing very well, and today our IPA sales are growing rapidly even in places where it has been available for much longer than a decade. In fact, according to a 2012 IRI grocery-scan data report, if you combine our IPA, our Maximus, and our Hop Stoopid, a very big chunk of all the IPAs sold in Northern California are Lagunitas.

Back when I started to wrap my mind around our IPA, there was another deeper brand-development idea at work in me. It was rooted in the dangerous idea that Sierra Nevada actually brewed their pale ale as a brand. Because our pale ale entered the market second, we could only ever hope to brew it as a style. You see, Sierra Nevada and pale ale are *one idea*. When people think of a pale ale, they think of Sierra Nevada. The same is true for Redhook and ESB, and for Widmer and hefeweizen. This meant that if Lagunitas brewed a pale ale—even if it was popular—every case sold of Lagunitas Pale Ale would only help to incrementally promote Sierra Nevada's pale by making the very concept of pale ale more popular.

One time, due to a dispute with our two distributors, Sierra Nevada's pale was taken off tap and our pale ale was put in its place. Instantly we were selling five kegs a week—more than any other account we had anywhere. I knew that this was not because we were so loved, but rather because people were ordering "pale ale" and expecting to get a Sierra Nevada beer. So in 1995 I knew that if Lagunitas could begin to brew our IPA as a genuine brand, then in the future, when other brewers made an IPA, we could benefit. Maybe. Possibly. You never know. This is one reason, among others, that the IPA graphic is so bold and plain on our label. So far, my dangerous assumption seems to be accurate, but it might take another decade or two to know for sure. The good news? I'm patient.

With all of this in mind, when we first introduced the Lagunitas IPA as a very separate product from our pale ale, we were able to price it higher and more closely to what it cost to produce. That was the beginning of Lagunitas becoming the premium-priced brand that we had really wanted and needed to be from the start. For a number of years we maintained two product price levels. Our pale ale and amber ale were at the $5.99 price, and our IPA and Pils were $6.99. We sold the snot out of the pale in bottles, and we pushed the IPA only in kegs. At a certain point we changed our bottle focus to only IPA and let the pale ale slowly fade. We had the Pils as the lager analog of the IPA, and it was somewhat groundbreaking in its own right. Even today, we are one of only a handful of craft brewers with the chops to brew a good (maybe great!?) pilsner. The Pils is hard and inconvenient to make, but it represents the highest art of brewing and earns us more than a little respect—in the world at large and in that all-important version: *self-respect*. In 2009 we placed third in the most prestigious of the European beer judging events. Imagine an American lager ranking third among the world's best lager brewers! Cool, it is.

With respect to basic pricing, to this day we rarely lead the category pricing, and instead I like to be at the "nice" end of the high-priced zone. But once again, uh, I digress . . .

During the late 1990s my printing biz stayed afloat, and more often than not I would receive big commission checks from printers, which would go directly to the brewery account, bypassing my personal account altogether. We'd take back only what we needed to buy food and keep the mortgage intact at home. This tactic avoided the explaining to my significant other where all the money was going, because in truth, I didn't yet completely understand the balance-sheet thing myself, although I was starting to get the idea. If you don't have a bank or enthusiastic shareholders, or wealthy parents or in-laws, then you have to get the money from profits alone, and those, while inadequate, were entirely absorbed by the inventory and receivables accounts on the balance sheet.

One spring, always a financially hard time because the big summer ramp-up in distributor inventories would begin, our growth sopped up all of the cash to such an extent that I could see a crisis coming. The crunch concluded in the unimaginable: we did not have enough cash for payroll. In all the years of tough financial times, we had never, ever missed a payroll. That would have been like using a Bible for kindling, or smoking in a cancer ward. Payroll is the highest sacred trust in running a business. I didn't have any way to raise cash quickly, so cutting expenses was the only way out. I decided that if I shut down the brewery for one pay period, saving that one payroll would amount to a small cash infusion. Small, but enough to get us through to enter the summer's sales levels in order to reenergize the business's finances.

I called a company meeting and tried—badly, as it turned out—to explain the inventory/receivables/cash thing to the crew. I say "badly" because my little speech became a sort of standing joke among the brewers and bottlers (and my bookkeeper) for several years afterward. I thought the little metaphors I made up about "too little oil in the oil pan" and "rapid acceleration" were illuminating, but they weren't, and in the end it didn't matter. Everybody kinda nodded and blinked and later laughed, and a school's-out atmosphere filled the brewery as we shut down. Instead of being seen as a treasonous crime, everybody thought it was fine, and about two-thirds of the crew, especially those responsible for fermentation control, cleaning machines, maintenance, accounting, and sales, all came in to work anyway. I felt terrible and humbled and grateful at the same time. That was the first time I really understood how much community was evolving around the business and Lagunitas as a company. The whole thing scared the hell out of me for a while, but in the end it was a positive learning experience.

When my printing biz inevitably evaporated from neglect in favor of the brewery, I turned to our house for liquidity. It was during the very earliest days of the liberalizing of the mortgage business. I did not know why at the time, but my bank seemed more than willing to continuously refinance my house if I fixed up parts of it enough to move the needle on the appraisal even slightly. Once I got the hang of it, I would purloin a few thousand dollars from the brewery to fix up a bathroom, have it reappraised, slip the appraiser a couple of cases of beer, yuck it up a bit with him, get the appraisal up by $50,000, borrow back the revised maximum loan to value metric, and—presto!—$3,000 in diverted cash flow became $40,000 in new working capital for the brewery. It seemed like magic. From a post-sub-prime-meltdown perspective, it was!

At one point early on in 1996, we enjoyed a lot of preliminary attention from what was then the largest bank in California. Seems they'd had some very good experience with another very large California brewer, and they developed a thirst for hops. They assigned a senior loan officer in Santa Rosa to identify breweries that appeared to have the "right stuff" and to begin to develop lending/deposit relationships with them. We were on their radar, and they did a couple of modest equipment loans with us. I wanted to go all the way with them and really recapitalize the brewery, so we initiated the process for a big SBA loan. They were excited, and I was as giddy as a sixteen-year-old girl.

But (and there always seemed to be a big *but* somewhere) while we were doing well and growing skinny, another more established brewery up north of us was also deeply involved with the same bank, but for them, events were skidding sideways. I was later told a story by a senior guy at that bank about a $1 million line of credit that the other brewery was in danger of defaulting on. As can be the case with big-bank logic, their internal analysts decided that if one brewery could have such troubles, the whole category could be doomed. In truth, that was 1996, and the industry was entering a time of significant oversupply and closures, but none of that ever touched us.

Finally, after seven months of endless paperwork requests from the big bank with regard to the SBA loan—paperwork requests that I started to think were designed just to make us go away—the big bank would only part with a fraction of the requested amount for the mostly federally guaranteed SBA loan. The big bank finally made that small loan, but to do it they tied up almost $1 million in business and personal assets as security for the $80,000 of comparatively expensive five-year financing. The loan was something, and by the time it actually funded, we really needed it, but it was not nearly enough to make us strong, and so things continued hand-to-mouth. Over time, I wore out my house as a capital source. In fact, when we finally sold the house in 2002, we sold it for $100,000 less than the most recent appraisal. I guess I had been a good salesman when it came to entertaining the appraisers.

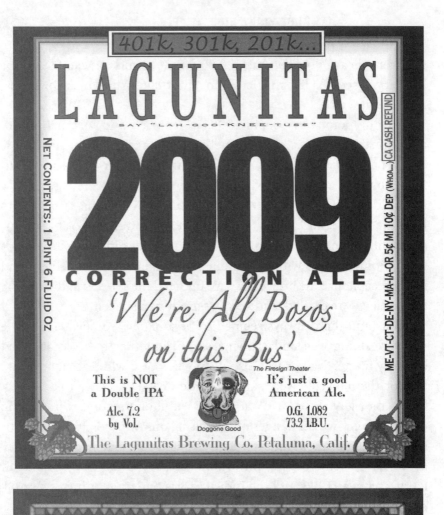

LAGUNITAS

SAY "LAH-GOO-KNEE-TUSS"

2009

CORRECTION ALE

'We're All Bozos
on this Bus'

The Firesign Theater

This is NOT
a Double IPA

It's just a good
American Ale.

Alc. 7.2
by Vol.

O.G. 1.082
73.2 I.B.U.

Doggone Good

The Lagunitas Brewing Co. Petaluma, Calif.

NET CONTENTS: 1 PINT 6 FLUID OZ

ME-VT-CT-DE-NY-MA-IA-OR 5¢ MI 10¢ DEP (WHOA...)CA CASH REFUND

I THINK WE'RE ALL BOZOS ON THIS BUS... I mean, really; who would ever have given their money to a guy with a name like 'Made-Off'? If one day an oily guy named Soprano showed up at your door wearing a suit that said 'Countrywide' offering free money; who would have taken it? Isn't 'free money' an oxymoron? If it was all too good to be true, it was. Wasn't the end in sight when 'Flip This House' went on television...? In the future 2009 will be in there with 1929, 1941, and 1968. *OK*, we *all* partied down and, *yes*, we took some liberties with some of our female guests. But now it's the day after Mardi Gras when everyone kneels down and prays. Apparently, it really is possible to have too much fun. But it is far better to have partied and lost than never to have partied at all. Gracefully surrender the things of 2008. So, smoke a fag, drink a beer, and buy toothpaste...in that order. Live to party again.

CREATIVE FUNDING

ROBBING PETER TO PAY PAUL

By 1998 I realized that we would need to start thinking about relocating the brewery once again. We were occupying most of the small and compartmented building that we were in, and we had almost no floor left. Drains and the six-inch-thick slabs seemed in danger of failing altogether under the hundreds of thousands of pounds of beer-filled fermentation and bottling tanks. By that time we had an accountant, mostly for taxes, and together we decided that we needed to raise some money, and that if we were going to take that step, we should also move to a bigger space at the same time. We put together a good prospectus and business plan (none of the things shown in the plan ever occurred as planned, of course). This would be Lagunitas's third home and fourth brew house in five years, and we were yet to have a year with positive cash flow, let alone a meaningful profit.

From 1992 until 1997 I had paid my personal income taxes one year late every single year. The first year was the sort of cat-and-mouse game that you would imagine; they really wanted their money. I was starting to rebuild some printing work, so I had some income again, and I was dealing with the 1-800-IRS phone attendants, who have no latitude. When I would promise to make a payment by a certain date and I couldn't do it because a commission check from a printing project hadn't arrived on time, the IRS would immediately empty my personal checking account and bounce my defaulting mortgage or car payment or whatever. I was willing to pay, but they were so capricious that I figured it was war. So over the course of 1993 I opened a dozen different bank accounts so that the money would be harder to find, and as the net grew tighter, I began moving checks around daily. Something like this: I'd deposit a check for X dollars in Bank A, then I'd walk down the street to Bank B and deposit a check from Bank A for the same uncollected and freshly deposited X dollars. I'd repeat this up and down the block between the banks, arriving back at Bank A again, where I'd rewrite that same check. The deposits would all reconcile the next morning, and if the IRS or California tried to get the money, some other bank would already have earmarked it for transfer. I thought it was pretty clever.

Truth is, banking was not nearly as efficient in the backrooms as it is today, and the banks I was using were mostly small mom-and-pops, so they were inclined to be more friendly than suspicious. But it was genuine check kiting! Finally, one of the banks detected the "unusual movement," closed my account, and notified the other banks too. It was pretty crazy.

During the third year of the income-tax lateness, I got a little wiser. Here's what I learned about how the IRS does what it does: if you have a problem, and you don't have the money that you owe on April 15, file anyway. Forty-five days later they will send you a letter demanding the dough. Take the letter and smoke it. Don't answer! If you do, you will end up talking to very menial 1-800–type attendants who will push a little button on their screen and start a sinister timer running. There will be no negotiating. Instead, if you can stand it, wait until you get the fifth letter around September. It will come via certified mail. Answer that one right away. That letter will have a different phone number on it that rings into a Seattle office called the ACS (Automated Collection Service, but it is not automated at all). The hold music is Vivaldi, and it will drive you crazy. Eventually you will speak to a person who can make deals. Not on the amount, but on the terms. Make them a promise, and then, by all means, keep it. If you can't keep it, call the day before and tell them. They won't like it, but if you keep up your end of the deal—which includes telling them *before* you are late—they will keep up their end of the deal too. No more seizing bank accounts. If you don't want to wait for the fifth letter, call me. I kept the secret ACS phone number just in case.

If you're keeping score, then you have guessed that instead of catching up and paying my taxes on time, I was putting all of my money back into the brewery. That is correct: even though no bank would step up and fund a growing business because of its immaturity, the IRS did! Of course, they didn't know they were funding my growing brewery, but it seems like they might have agreed to it if they had been disposed to consider it. The interest rate they charge on unpaid taxes is better than any bank would have offered me, and the "loan" helped support the brewery's cash flow and ultimately helped to generate the remittance of millions of dollars of my current and future employees' income taxes as well as many, many more millions in future excise-tax payments. It was a classic win-win.

By 1997, even though I was still not on payroll myself (although we did have ten or twelve others on payroll by then), the brewery had sufficient cash flow for me to make a payment arrangement with the IRS. The amount owed had grown because our little brewery was still a sole proprietorship, and so our total revenue appeared on my own household Schedule C return. It looked pretty impressive to file (my alleged gross income was something like $1.3 million!), but it made me owe a *lot* more income tax. It would be $1,942 per month for three years, and then I was even.

But once again, I, well, uh, digress . . .

So I went to the private world for money in July 1998. That project was a high-wire act for me. I was not very sophisticated, and I quickly learned that even pausing to take a breath during a presentation was enough to scare off an investor. Weakness and hesitancy are not tolerated in this world. When I would make a good presentation, we'd shake hands firmly. I'd leave with some optimism, go to my car, and instantly fall hard asleep. It was the most stressful thing ever, and during that time, with the exception of when in my car, I permanently forgot how to sleep well. That was true largely because the plan we set in motion included forward commitments to buy equipment, lease space, engage contractors, and put every piece in place without any way to pay for all of those promises if I did not manage to raise the money. It was like being on a speeding train with no brakes and knowing that up ahead they were still working on building the bridge across the gorge.

I had originally set out to find investments from just a couple of local guys-done-good, but the dot-com and telecom bubble had not yet burst, so all the money was then going to those kinds of companies. Instead, I was able to raise money from friends and friends of friends in mostly small chunks. My future landlord, Mike Buckley, put in a good-sized portion. He agreed to it one morning during a very plain two-hour conversation—our first meeting—without any haggling or posturing. There was no "I'll need to think about it" or "Let me discuss it with my accountant or wife." There was just a simple "This looks good. I like the beer; it seems like it'll be fun." Thus began the most straightforward and integrity-based relationship that the business or I ever have enjoyed. In that sort of relationship it is so very easy to tell the unvarnished truth, good or hard, and know that you'll get useful feedback. Would that they were all like that. Mike has also ever since been the single most important business advisor, financial mentor, and fearless supporter of me personally and of the business. It was another of those "unbelievably right thing at the perfect moment" events that dot the landscape of the brewery's history.

On the family side, only my father-in-law came aboard for a little bit of the action. It was very cool that he wanted in, although I think he really just wanted to know about the adventure firsthand.

By late 1998 I had made lots of commitments to equipment brokers and contractors and such, and failure to complete the capital raise was not an option, even though it was a distinct possibility. In the end, I was just barely able to raise the money we set out to find. On top of the competition from the stock-market bubble du jour, there was lots of bad news swirling around craft brewing, and we were still struggling toward profitability ourselves. The signed subscription agreements already in place included a deadline of December 31 for completing a minimum capital raise, and if I did not raise the minimum amount, I would have to return the money that I had collected up to that point. The lease I had signed began in February 1999; the thirty-barrel brew house was being disassembled and shipped to arrive in January 1999, the same for the new/used bottling line, a filter, fermenters, boilers, and so on. During one presentation I remember hammering a good guy for the last piece needed to make the minimum capital raise, and existentially hearing myself sounding like one of those soulless stock guys you see squeezing blue-haired dowagers for cash in bad Wall Street movies. That last chunk came through on December 27, and I got drunk.

When you are raising money in a challenged environment—as the late 1990s were—tiny things are magnified, if only to serve as a way to say no. One tiny thing that came up as a concern to prospective investors was that we owed our accountants a chunk of money from the development of the financial side of the business plan used in the equity raise. To fix this, I went to a very, very local bank where we had our deposit and checking accounts and asked for a small loan to retire that balance. I was summarily declined. It took them all of about three hours to make that decision. I didn't understand at all. I didn't understand banking, that is. I thought to myself, *We are an increasingly respected local brand showing strong growth, and we have all our deposit accounts at this bank.* I didn't know much about how the bank would look at us and our cash flow, or lack thereof. I only knew that if I borrowed the money, I'd pay it back. That seemed simple enough to me, but then I was still an ex–musician/printing salesman pretending to own a brewery. All ignorance aside, I was genuinely angry and frustrated. They were happy to accept our deposits and use that cash as an asset to leverage and lend to other businesses, but they wouldn't return the favor over a very small amount of credit. They even had big posters behind the tellers in every branch proclaiming their commitment to working with local businesses and serving their community. Whatever.

When they declined the credit, I gathered up all my self-righteous indignity and marched into the chief credit officer's office unannounced and had my say while standing over him seated at his desk.

He stared in disbelief like a deer in headlights while I declared that he was a fraud and that when he saw our deposit accounts close the next morning, he should intuit a one-to-one relationship between that and the decline of my recent credit request. I felt dramatic and strong, although I am pretty sure that I sounded ridiculous, but it was nonetheless satisfying. He blinked a banker's blink and calmly asked me if I was unhappy with the checking-account relationship. My jaw went sorta slack. I had meant to conclude the meeting by pissing on his desk, but his response confused me, and I forgot. To this very day, bankers are still impenetrable souls to me, with one important exception, but more on that later.

Robin McClain, controller and original bookkeeper

When I interviewed with Tony for a bookkeeping job I thought he was a strange guy. I asked him for $10 an hour (it was still 1995!) and he said no. I had gone to the interview determined not to take less so I got ready to leave. Then he said, "I have to give you $15." I said . . . "Oh?" He said, "I can't pay the bookkeeper less than anyone else or you might decide to take it yourself." Seriously? OK then, I'll see you Monday.

I drove into the parking lot of a tiny building in an industrial park, parking next to a small truck with paper piled on the dashboard two inches thick. I think to myself, *Gee, I hope that's not [Tony's] truck*. As I walked into the office, Tony looks at me like he had never seen me before. I said, "I'm the bookkeeper, remember?" He kind of fumbles around, moves some papers on a table, and says, "Here's where you will work." It was a table, a folding metal chair, and the smallest computer I had ever seen. I asked if I would be using that computer and he says, "The Mac's screen was 6" x 6"." I asked, "OK, where do you keep your receipts and bills?" He says "Oh . . . be right back." He walked out with a paper bag. I'm thinking, What have I gotten myself into? He walks back in with all those papers from his dashboard in a grocery bag and says, "You can start with this." This was supposed to be an eight-hour-a-week job. It never was.

Lagunitas has always been chaotic, fun, and challenging. We would all think, *Oh, it should slow down a little next year*, but it never did. I don't think any of us ever thought it would become what it is, certainly not for the first ten years. I actually expected a massive bankruptcy.

There were quite a few mornings in the first ten years when I didn't want to go to work because I didn't want to have to tell the vendors we couldn't pay them that week. Very few of them were nasty about it. Most everyone was understanding and most couldn't believe I was telling them the truth and not ignoring their calls.

I think Lagunitas's success is 50 percent Tony and 50 percent all the people he has hired and surrounded himself with over the years. His imagination is boundless. His organizational skills suck. That's why he needs all of us. The turnover of employees at Lagunitas is surprisingly small. I know a lot of us were underpaid and overworked for many years, but we all stayed. I think it was mostly because it felt like family. If you walked into Lagunitas, you would never know who the owner was. He might be talking to you but you would never know it, he would never tell you. I guess that's the part I like, and I think the world feels the same way.

LAGUNITAS

The first sip is for thirst, the second one for pleasure.

The third sip for romance, and the fourth for pure madness.

69.39 IBU

Olde GNARLYWINE Style Ale

O.G. 1.096   Alc. 9.7% vol.

NET CONTENTS 12 FL. OZ

BREWED AND BOTTLED BY LAGUNITAS BREWING CO. PETALUMA CALIF.

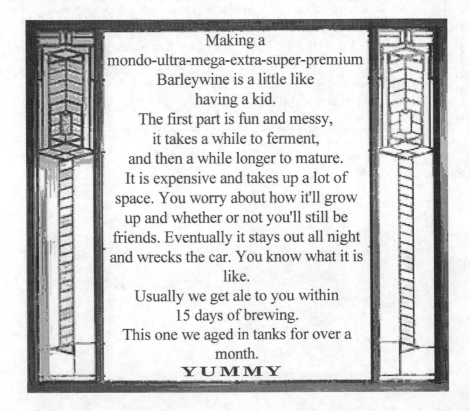

Making a mondo-ultra-mega-extra-super-premium Barleywine is a little like having a kid.
The first part is fun and messy, it takes a while to ferment, and then a while longer to mature.
It is expensive and takes up a lot of space. You worry about how it'll grow up and whether or not you'll still be friends. Eventually it stays out all night and wrecks the car. You know what it is like.
Usually we get ale to you within 15 days of brewing.
This one we aged in tanks for over a month.
YUMMY

DRAMAS AND DEBACLES

*I*n the course of the equity raise, I provided a stock grant to two employees to whom I'd made promises several years earlier. It was 1998, and we were in California, surrounded by dozens of high-tech-this and high-speed-that start-up companies, and it was the height of the dot-com bubble, so everybody everywhere seemed to be working for stock grants. By that time, the idea of going to work and earning a paycheck was almost quaint. As you all know by now, Lagunitas was not making any money, and while everybody wanted equity so that they could "eat what they kill," most people didn't want the responsibility of paying very much too far forward in order to see those future happy days. For the record, all during the couple of years after I made my promise to these employees, I continued to shovel my own paychecks into the company but never asked them to ante up like in a normal cash-call situation. So the 10 percent promise remained intact.

That original promise of 10 percent of the company was for when we would change from a sole proprietorship to an S corporation and issue share certificates, but within a year of that delivered promise, I had to raise more money. The expansion was more expensive than I thought it would be (for a change), and we grew quickly again (for a change). With the second equity raise, their 10 percent was diluted to about 7 percent, and the next round, a year later, diluted them further to less than 5 percent, and then with the last, most desperate round in 2003, it took them down to less than 1 percent each. My own ownership would have tanked along with theirs, except that with each round, I went to the bank and squeezed my house a little harder, and then a little harder, and then a little harder. By going deeper into debt personally, I was able to hang on to control of my company in the hopes that someday I'd be able to climb back out of the hole.

But the dilution rubbed the two employees to whom I had provided the stock grant the wrong way. One of them had his father call our attorney and demand that he be put on the board of directors and that I issue additional shares to him in order to restore his "ownership interest." I didn't have any legal obligation to do that, and we told him so. Without even taking a breath, the dad told us he would litigate. My attorney (the soulful kind that defies all the labels) closed the folder in front of him and declared, "You have your remedies." He then stood up and left the dad and son in his conference room, and my wife and I filed out behind him, a little ashen-faced.

That was the end of that chapter until 2010, when I finally was able to buy that employee's shares back from his dad. As it turned out, when the company became profitable, his son began to owe taxes on that profitability, which he could not pay, so his dad paid the taxes for him and took the shares in compensation.

The second remaining employee wanted to live more like his own mental image of a business owner, and that included taking a whole lot of time off. He was generally unhappy and finally quit one afternoon in 2002, demanding that I buy his shares back on the spot. Unfortunately for him, he had agreed to a standard small-company share-buyback agreement under which, if he left the company, the fair value of the shares would be determined by a simple balance-sheet calculation. The bad news was that, because of our financial ill health, that value was a negative number! So after trying a few bits of cleverness to try to lever a different result from me, he surrendered his shares and went on his way.

My five-year-old handshake with them was always good, and I gave them the shares as promised, but they were not really prepared to understand what they had asked for and what obligations would come along with it all. To be truthful, when I offered them the shares, I did not fully understand it all either, but the time and experience and resolve to see the thing through required me to learn what I had to learn so that I could protect the business and shepherd it safely into its future. The whole series of events was difficult for me, and I felt bad about the way it turned out for those two guys, but at the time I didn't have the money to be generous and relieve them of the circumstance that they were in. If they were children, it might have been different, but we were all grown-ups. Let me close this sad scene by saying that you should never have partners who don't have as much to lose as you do, and you should never, ever, ever give equity to employees without a meaningful vesting period. Word.

There were many dramas, large and small, that occurred during the course of the actual move to the new building in February 1998. Two were particularly scary.

The first: as we were just about to move the office and accounting departments, something strange happened to our accounting software. It made a funny face and asked us to phone home for its mama. We did, and its mama was as unhelpful as could be. In the course of starting up the computer one fine morning, we had lost all of our accounting information. The software maker told us that an "interrupted save" was to blame. They said it was our problem and that nothing could be done. Seems that when we reloaded our backups, they somehow caught the same disease and died as well. My bookkeeper stared at me aghast. At that point, I really didn't know anything about double-entry accounting; I was a designer and brewer, at best. In my whole thirty-eight years on earth I had never even balanced my own personal checkbook. I had no idea how hard or how long it was going to take to rebuild the accounts and produce financial reports, but I could tell that my bookkeeper did. The look on her face was that of somebody looking up while falling backward into a very, very deep hole.

Reassembling our finances ended up taking from February to December. It took forever because the brewery was a galloping

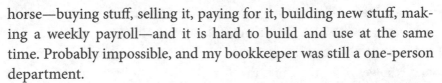

horse—buying stuff, selling it, paying for it, building new stuff, making a weekly payroll—and it is hard to build and use at the same time. Probably impossible, and my bookkeeper was still a one-person department.

The second scary thing: my bookkeeper dove headfirst into rebuilding the financial accounting, and then she began getting a divorce too. In the course of rebuilding it all, she still closed out each month the best she could, but every month there would be "general journal" entries made to resolve something that had come to light from previous months as we were trying to perfect the opening balances from a year prior on the back of that galloping horse. This meant that the interim statements were essentially meaningless, because of all the "adjustments." At the same time, we seemed to be going through the remainder of the raised capital a little bit quickly because of having to pay bills, but there was no way to know what was going on. By that point, the horse was galloping backward, downhill, on a rough road, with its eyes closed, in the middle of a whiteout snowstorm, and there was a great fear that the road might come to an end.

At the time, I had a long-standing plan to help a friend bring a sailboat home from Hawaii in August after a race, and I was looking forward to the big break after the intensity of the capital raise and the move. I would be gone for a month—my first such time off since the brewery began. When I got back to the office one sunny Monday in September, there was a crisp-looking set of financial statements on my desk from August. I assumed that things at the brewery would be as good as I felt in that moment. I picked up the statements and automatically flipped to the last page of the income statement.

Due to some substantial general journal entries (the "adjustments" I mentioned earlier) that had to be made to accurately report expenses from earlier in the year (though I would only learn that later), there were strange red symbols on the bottom line of the income statement that I was sure couldn't be numbers as I knew them. I don't know exactly what a heart attack feels like, but I'm sure my heart stopped. Thinking quickly, I began beating myself on the chest and head with my fists and coughed up something that looked like a lung. Looking up, everything turned to black and white, and then, mercifully, I passed out.

When I woke up I was back in Hawaii, but only for an instant. I reached up from the floor, blindly fumbled around my desktop for the income statement, and dragged it down under my desk, where I tried again to read it.

We had lost money that month, I was sorta used to that, but this loss was roughly equal to the total sales for the month. We sold about $110,000 in beer and somehow lost about that much too. I had to ask a lot of questions before I understood that what had happened was an "accounting adjustment" and not the end of the world as I'd known it. I survived that moment, and as the next few years passed, I became more comfortable dealing with those kinds of numbers. Today I also drag race, skydive, bungee jump, free-climb, drink lye, handle snakes, and swallow swords each morning before work.

But my digression digresses.

In 1999 we finally completed the capital raise; installed the new/used brew house, the additional tanks, the new/used bottling line, a new/used refrigeration system, more new/used kegs, and a new/used boiler; did the building renovations; moved into the new brewery; and so on. We used some of the new capital for the gear, but to preserve as much of the cash as possible, I mostly financed the stuff with application-only leases.

At that moment I was a brain-dead bona fide sucker. Since we still did not have a strong financial inventory and receivables position, we still did not have a bank. In fact, we would not establish a real banking relationship for another six or seven years. I wanted to preserve as much of the cash raised as possible for future working capital needs (remember inventory and receivables?), so I decided that, since I had a pretty good personal credit score, I would get the leases myself.

Because I didn't understand how leases were actually structured, I considered only the monthly payments when it came to the decision. This is how they sell you a car lease: "Hi, Mister Magee! What would you say if I told you I could put you behind the wheel of this shiny new AMC Pacer for only $349 per month*? (*Plus .25/mile over 300 miles/

year and a residual value of twice the purchase price)." We had cash in the bank, and the business was growing fast, so I felt (overly) confident. It turned out later that the leases I signed had "effective" annual interest rates of 18 percent and 24 percent. That placed an enormous cash burden on the brewery for the five-year term of most of the leases. We made do on the plant side. We substituted creativity for money; wages were low; the lighting was terrible; my own income went to its lowest point in more than ten years; we paid bills late—some *very* late.

During the period of 1999 through 2005, I needed to raise smaller chunks of capital a number of times to keep the ship's rail above water. We were always growing, but as you understand by now, if you don't start out with enough money, growth causes its own variety of problems. This is what I mean when I say I felt like I was being chased down the street by a pack of rabid wild dogs. If I slowed down my running for even a moment to look behind me, I was doomed. I had to raise money, we had to manage our payables relationships, and we had to grow.

At one point in the late 1990s we were pretty dog-desperate for some cash relief, and a printing friend of mine suggested that I could change my receivables terms and have a one-time acceleration in our cash receipts. I guess it is a pretty basic concept, but I had never thought of the "time value" of money in that simple way before. It was a great idea, and our distributors were willing, since most took a delivery at least every week, and so they were turning their inventories around fast, and yet I had been allowing them to float each cash sale for another few weeks. They were on board, and we got a little moment of relief, but we needed more.

So we opened a conversation with a really bad—no, a *really evil*—bank out of San Jose that set me up in the worst straitjacket I'd ever worn. It was a receivables line of credit in name only. It was actually the most brutal form of factoring ever. It turned out to be very restrictive, and very expensive, and the bank was astoundingly careless in its calculation of our cash receipts and our available cash (for paying our bills and making payroll). We got very sick of the arrangement very quickly. But extricating ourselves from it was difficult. When the bank

> ## Bob Brader, Tony's Brother-in-Law
>
> What did those first brews taste like? I think it would be easier to describe what Tony's first beers did not taste like . . . they did not taste like beer. There were many different colors, textures, tastes, and alcohol levels, and who knows what was floating in the bottle. But Tony and Carissa worked every day, doing whatever it took to make sure they were still in business tomorrow. They sacrificed for years. Tony's vision, uncompromising commitment to brand, and consistent quality and fun are what made Lagunitas a success. Everyone I talk to who has bought the beer loves the stories on the boxes and bottles. Where does Tony get that stuff? My favorite beer so far is Maximus.

figured out that we were reducing our use of the available credit and untangling ourselves from the credit facility, they got angry. After all, Tony Soprano doesn't actually want you to pay off your debt to him; he just wants you to service it. The bank demanded that I sign a bunch of releases to give them access to our tax reporting for another five years. I was planning on pulling the plug soon and refused to sign it. They got even more angry and threatening, and although I offered to sign for the then-current term of our agreement with them, they arbitrarily demanded the five years.

I'll never forget the moment, driving across the San Mateo Bridge, talking to the bank guy on my cell phone. When I said no, I would not sign the releases, this diminutive bankeroid said lightly, "Oh, OK, have it your way." I kinda wondered what would happen next, but I turned to my friend, and we lit up. A frantic call from my bookkeeper some twenty minutes later told me that the bastard had put down the phone and frozen our line of credit, strangling the business and the forthcoming paychecks of all of its employees (and their families) and instantly cutting us off from any of our own cash receipts until we came into compliance, or at least bent over and accepted his discipline.

The unilateralism was stunning, and I felt a murderous rage rising. Payroll was the next day, we needed a glass delivery, and grain bills and rent were soon due. Our relationship with the bank had to end.

Despite my feelings otherwise, I figured that it would be better for everyone if the banker were still alive at the endpoint. This came a few weeks later, and as far as I know, he's still alive. If he's not, all I can say is, I didn't do it. It was a very bad experience, and I would never have thought that I could weave us into something so one-sided and brutal so easily. I had no idea what I was doing, and if you don't think those kinds of deals exist outside of Baghdad or Jersey City (no offense to Jersey City!), you're wrong. I've been very careful whom we do business with ever since.

If you recall the inventory-and-receivables concept of needing cash to pay bills before you collect for the stuff you have sold, then you know why Lagunitas's bills often got paid late. We were becoming profitable on paper, but we were still using more cash than we were generating. Some bills we could pay late, and some we could not. My strategy was to pay the majority of our bills on time, but when the money would run out each week, I would always pay one particular bigger supplier late. It also happened to be our single biggest raw-material bill each week. Since our other suppliers were mostly paid on time, all of the missing cash was focused into the amount we owed that one supplier.

The man who ran that company was actually a very good guy. He had taken over the business from his dad. I never knew his dad, but I suspect he was a pretty savvy and cagey man. He created a small monopoly and operated it as such. I don't think the son understood how straitjacketed his customers were used to feeling when he took over the company, and so he didn't understand why some felt as they did about his business. Sorta like a good prince who inherits his despotic father's kingdom and then doesn't understand why he is despised. No matter the reason, they were the single most important supplier to craft brewers who bottled their beer, and everybody was careful about maintaining good relations with them. Anyway, he had a mixed reputation in the industry, but I worked hard to get to know the guy who owned the supply business, and to make sure that he knew me. I believe in the "If you want to dislike someone, don't get to know them" idea, and I hoped it would work in reverse as well.

I also made sure that he knew me *and* the brewery, inside and out. I showed him how strong the brand was performing in the market, which was a very different thing from how strong the bank account was. By that time, in the late 1990s, we really were the strongest-growing brewery in percentage terms in Northern California—even one of the strongest growing in the whole damn country. Others were bigger, but we were on a tear! I made sure that I was always available to talk to him when he called. I would make biannual appointments to take him to lunch and show him our current financials and discuss my brand's Nielsen and IRI market rankings. I would bring paid aging reports so that he could see that he was the only supplier with whom I was so upside down. I explained that that meant that no one else could make demands on me that would interfere with my commitment to him.

Sometimes he would call and tell me that he needed me to make a large payment—$50,000, $100,000—and I never asked why. My bookkeeper would come into my office and tell me that particular vendor was on line two, and I would feel 280 volts automatically move from my brain stem to my shoulders and across my chest. I'd take a very deep breath, engineer a convincing smile, and reach for the phone. I would steal the quarters out of the company pop machine if I had to in order to be responsive to his requests. I believe that because of this, he was willing at other times to extend even more rope to me when I needed it. In reality, he'd allowed me enough to totally hang myself, but I didn't.

There was one other guy I always owed money to: the owner of our local trucking company. He ran a pretty big operation, but he did all the dispatching himself. He was a rock-solid guy, and his drivers loved and feared him. From time to time when we would call to schedule a pickup, he would mention that his accountants were telling him to scrub us off, that he didn't need our business, and that our slow pay status was costing him too much money. After all, he had payroll and fuel and truck payments himself. But he was way, way cool with us for some happy reason. He'd ask us to get a little more current, and we would, with gratitude, but eventually we'd fall behind again. He still does all of our local shipping, and there is a lot of it, and now we pay every invoice on time. He is, well, it is like he is proud of having helped us when we needed help, and now he reminds his accountants why he helped us out when they add up the nice profits he gets from our business today. He grew himself a good customer! That is a cool relationship.

About the same time as we were still slow-paying those two individuals, we had an employee—a really good, young guy—who was diagnosed with leukemia. It was terrible and it didn't go well for him, and after some last-chance experimental therapy in Texas, they told him there was nothing else to do. He couldn't get by without bottled oxygen, and so he wouldn't be allowed on a commercial jetliner. The drive back from Texas would have been too much for him physically, and that left chartering a private jet as his only way to get home to California to die. His family could not afford it, and of course the soulless ass-wipes at the insurance company told him to die in Texas. We were in financially desperate straits ourselves, but it was that handshake thing again. You make a promise when someone works hard for you, and so we enlisted a private jet company and said, "Fly him home." I called the supplier to whom I already owed so much and told him I needed a mulligan on that week's payment, and I told him why. He immediately said, "Yes, pay me later." Like I said earlier, he was actually a very good guy. In the end, the jet company never sent us a bill for the trip, and I don't think it was an oversight.

There is an old adage that if you owe your banker five hundred dollars and can't pay, you have a problem. But if you owe your banker $1 million and you can't pay, then your banker has a problem! (That is why two of our more recent presidents gave Wall Street whatever they wanted.) At one point, the big payable supplier asked me, with a funny tone in his voice, if that was how our relationship was structured too. That was the day my payables/funding strategy hit its limit. Happily, that coincided with our ability to begin to set things straight. I don't think his company ever acted as lenient with any other brewery, and I still feel indebted to him personally, even though I realized later that his company was very predatory with respect to pricing and was probably a drag on our whole West Coast craft-brewing industry. In any case, he did carry our large account payable ($500,000+ at an 18 percent annual interest rate!), and when the brewery finally became profitable, it happened in a big way, and we retired that debt quickly.

Business relationships often seem to overlap with personal relationships in uncomfortable and conflicting ways. They say that countries don't have friends—they have interests. While it's true that businesses share that reality, it is hard to play rough with people you have gotten to know and like and who have helped you, but I have always had employees who have committed themselves to me and the business, and I need to look out for them and our collective future before I think about my own relationships. The two are knitted together in ways that are not very clear until a conflict arises.

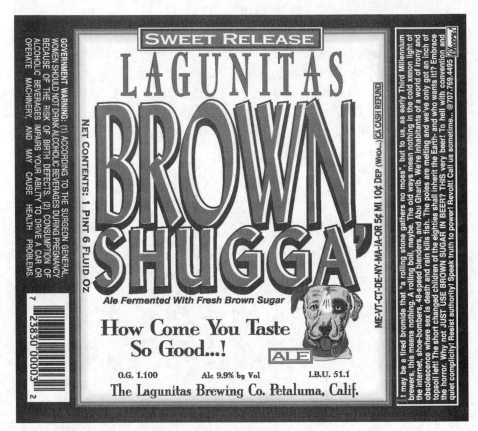

NET CONTENTS: 1 PINT 6 FLUID OZ

SWEET RELEASE

LAGUNITAS
BROWN SHUGGA'

Ale Fermented With Fresh Brown Sugar

How Come You Taste So Good...!

ALE

O.G. 1.100   Alc 9.9% by Vol   I.B.U. 51.1

The Lagunitas Brewing Co. Petaluma, Calif.

ME-VT-CT-DE-NY-MA-IA-OR 5¢ MI 10¢ DEP (WHOA....) CA CASH REFUND

It may be a 'tired bromide that "a rolling stone gathers no moss", but to us, as early Third Millennium brewers, this means nothing. A rolling boil, maybe. The old ways mean nothing in the cold xenon light of the internet, shoe-bombers, 48-speed blenders, and Abu Gharib. We're inhabitants of a world of irony and obsolescence where sex is death and rain kills fish. The poles are melting and we've only got an inch of topsoil left! The short changed children of the eighties shall inherit the Earth- and who wants it!? Embrace the horror. Why not JUST USE BROWN SUGAR IN BEER? THIS very beer! To hell with convention and quiet complicity! Resist authority! Speak truth to power! Revolt! Call us sometime.. @707.769.4495

First Brewed in October, 1996

As we brew this Special Ale in this the fourth part of the third year of a new and, so far, difficult millennuim we are thinking about how complicated our world has become and about how the space between us all sometimes grows. We hope this Ale and this Holiday Season find you and the ones closest to you in moments of quiesence from which new intimacies may arise. Maybe a new appreciation of a lifetimes unceasing ars will appear to you as real and as gently as a familiar voice might whisper in your ear. Maybe it's not really just Wendesday or Thirsday or today or yesterday or just now or just then... maybe it's all just plain 'mow' and maybe it's all we've gotand maybe that really is enough. Bring on then this time of the year when the skys sometimes cloud over and the wind and the rain drive us inside and together and for you may the shelter be as much about the roofs and walls as it is about the company and the shared time. Oh yes, and also the shared brews, but we've taken care of that.... Thanks for inviting us inside as well!

TRIED AND TESTED

THE ART OF STAYING AHEAD OF THE GAME

By fall 2003 we began to retire all of the crummy expensive leases that had held us down for the previous five years. Earlier that spring I had called three of the midsized local banks (but not that one who earlier told us to take a hike!) and invited them to come to the brewery so that I could show them our current financial situation, which was essentially this.

1. We were loaded with expensive but currently serviced debt.

2. Nearly all of that debt would mature in the next eight months.

3. Our accounts payable were upside down, but to only one supplier.

4. Our bottling line wasted 5 to 8 percent of the beer that we produced.

I contrasted this hard operational reality with our strong and thriving market position. I showed them what we had survived. We had been tested and had proven ourselves tough competitors. I made up a crisp financial model of what our world would look like if we restructured that big account payable at more realistic market rates (we were paying 18 percent interest on the over-terms portion). And most important, I showed them what would happen to our financials if we bought a new bottling line.

The "being tested" thing actually meant a lot to the bank. A small growing business that is full of its own success is not nearly as attractive as one that has seen hard times and prevailed through them. It's nice to know all the blood, sweat, and tears counted for more than just good experience.

Our existing bottling line was built in the 1960s to fill soda pop. It was seriously worn out by 2003, and 5 to 8 percent of the finished beer that went into it ended up being dumped because of broken bottles, bent caps, or short-filled bottles. If the bank lent us $1 million (gak!), I could buy a groovy new bottling line that would waste nothing, and all that extra beer would go out the door and be sold. The numbers were crazy: the bottling line financing would cost $16,000 per month, and the extra beer sold would create an additional $65,000 at no additional cost. If they financed this new bottling system, they would unlock enough margin for us then to replace the upstream filtration system with a similar positive-cash-flow effect, and that new combined profitability would later pay for a new brew house . . . and they could lend us all of that too. It seemed like magic.

Remember, for a bank, loans are assets, and making loans is how they make money. If the first loan could be made and the new profitability unlocked by the new bottle filler occurred as projected, then the bank could make all that other future business possible for themselves too. And for Lagunitas, we could have the best possible equipment so the quality of the beer would go through the roof.

Which is exactly what happened.

There is one other nasty thing about the brewery's finances that I should mention. We were servicing the giant account payable to the one supplier at 18 percent interest. The bank would be thrilled to earn even 7 percent on it, and the difference (11 percent) would return to the bottom line for us to spend on improvements or on keeping our beer prices low. It would be great business for us *and* great business for the bank. I could redo the entire brewery, and we would essentially get all of our equipment for free, since replacing any of it unlocked profit three to four times the value of the monthly payment. Think about it. It is a bent example of recursive self-improvement.

Once we were even-steven (from a debt perspective) with that most important supplier—our packaging supplier—we could start to discuss the pricing they had unilaterally imposed on us. The thing was, there was really only one supplier on the whole West Coast for the particular things we bought from them. (Packaging material was most of the cost of the beer that you bought in those days, although since that time malted barley and hops prices have gone up so much that they are now the most expensive ingredients, which makes more sense.) But because we were always behind on payments and I didn't want to bite the hand that fed me, I had never challenged the pricing of the packaging supplies. And in any case, there was no other option.

They had a lock on the supply, and the best carrier guys and the best glass guys and the best everything-else guys wouldn't sell to us directly—only through this dealer. It turned out that it was because the dealer protected these suppliers from having to compete on price, because the dealer would wrap up all of their individual components and sell a complete package. After some hard work, with a careful strategy, we were able to lever open a doorway to those other suppliers, one at a time, and our costs dropped dramatically. It's not like we got rich, because the business had other needs that were being starved while our trusted supplier was siphoning off so much of our cash. I once read a Harvard Business School paper that defined competition as "any entity that competes for your money, including substitute products, retailers, distributors and suppliers." It seemed that our biggest competition was our most important supplier. At one point, through the statewide brewers group, we even hosted a "packaging materials" presentation at the brewery to show other brewers what we had discovered and what we had accomplished, but while it was a full house, none broke away from the pack. There is a lot of fear that surrounds the unknown.

During that crazy period—on the heels of the later-to-be-described St. Patrick's Day Massacre, and during the lead-up to the specification work for the new bottling line—I got a call from a guy who was offering bottling line and purchasing consultation. He had worked for twenty-five years for the best brewery in our entire industry and had retired a year earlier. He was looking for clients, and it seemed that other small brewers saw him as some sort of charlatan, so customers were not readily forthcoming. I couldn't believe that this person—an unrecognized hero I'd never heard of, an individual who'd been to the freakin' mountaintop and was offering his experience to us, a guy who'd seen the glory of the comin' of the Lord, a person who could show me how to use our minor purchasing leverage to unlock stronger operating margins—could be hired at all, and was on hold on line two. I tried then, and have tried every week since then, to hire him on to the brewery full-time. Alas, he prefers consulting, but his insight has transformed my understanding of how to make a brewery earn money with reasonable pricing and how to leverage our minor purchasing influence to obtain enormous improvements in our raw materials costs. To top it all off, we have even become friends.

But well, you know, again, uh, I digress . . .

So at the end of that summer of 2003, as we retired the various leases, I got back in touch with the three midsized local banks that I had invited to the brewery earlier that year. It was like *Goldilocks and the Three Bears.* The first said no ("Maybe in ten years after you show us you don't need the money"). The second seemed just plain scared (and wouldn't return phone calls). But the third banker saw what I was talking about, and even more: a way to get 'er done, which he eventually did. It ended up being the next-most profoundly crucial relationship in the life of the brewery. He appeared on the scene at exactly the right moment. It isn't common to think of a banker as anything other than a penny-pinching guy with a green visor, beady eyes, and expensive shoes, but this good guy broke the mold.

The get-'er-done part, of course, did not turn out to be all that simple. A couple months after our meeting, the banker's employer was bought by a very unpleasant larger bank that had turned me down years earlier for a small car loan while I had four times the value of the car on deposit with them in our household account. So he and the whole damn loan department deserted ship en masse and opened an office across the street for an out-of-the-area bank that wanted to do business loans in our area. Perfect. The stars aligned. The bank was

> *Emil Kerputchinikinik, the original Lagunitas head brewer*
>
> I first met Magee drinking second-runnings Arkhi in Ulaanbaatar after the 1972 spring thaw. I didn't work for him then, and I wouldn't have done so later except that I still owed him for blowing the brain out of that old man back in Jabbachichma, and some people make it hard to resolve debts. And after all these years, has it paid off? In a way, I guess, like, well . . . I haven't accidentally found myself sober in years. The whole craft brewing movement reminds me of a Philistine uprising . . . doomed and sad. But it's too late for me . . . already having drunk the Kool-Aid and all. And, by Kool-Aid, I mean that mess they call the Maximus Ale.

hungry, a guy who understood us was in a senior seat, and we were ready to live up to the opportunity. In 2004 the new bank financed our new bottling line. The next year they financed thousands of new kegs, a dozen new three-hundred- and five-hundred-barrel fermenters, a state-of-the-art high speed centrifuge, new refrigeration stuff, a new coffeemaker, better lighting, other stuff, things, parts, pieces, you name it.

The brewery was firing on all cylinders, and between 2004 and 2008 we eventually succeeded in finally rebuilding it from stem to stern with truly state-of-the-art brewing gear. There's that sexy gear thing again! Now we genuinely have the most advanced brew house and filtration systems installed in any craft brewery in the country, maybe the world. Not the biggest, but the best.

By 2007 the real-estate bubble began to sag and our shiny new bank started to sag too. We submitted a financing request for the planned purchase of some new kegs. Our banker said it would be straightforward to fund, but then the senior bank-folk declined it. The rejection was a shock for us, because we could well afford the financing, and it was a shock to the loan officer for the same reason. To make things a little more complicated, $500,000 worth of kegs were already on a container ship to us from Spain. We were able to quickly obtain financing through another bank, but our existing relationship was seriously in question. So unwarranted was the credit decline that my friend the loan officer actually resigned his division presidency over it. The bank's chief credit officer later flew down to meet with us. Everyone on our side of the table agreed that he looked like he'd been pulled through a knothole a few times. Turns out the bank was bleeding badly over some troubled real-estate business, and they wanted to gently get rid of us, their single big customer, in order to instead have a dozen smaller customers replace us, their combined indebtedness equaling ours. That would have allowed the bank to impose separate fees on each of the smaller customers, and probably higher interest rates as well. What a world, what a world. Since then, I've heard that the bank's fortunes (or lack thereof) have become even more complicated.

But our loan officer remained a friend of mine and of our business and its future (in both of our interests), and he landed an even more senior position at a larger and, at the time, way stronger institution. Check this out: the new larger bank had attempted to buy our old (troubled) bank a couple of years earlier, and in the course of their due diligence, had carefully reviewed our loan file as a sample of the target bank's underwriting thoroughness. It seems that they liked what they saw about us even then. They put together a very aggressive offer and in early 2008 took over all of our banking business. In the world of small circles and narrow degrees of separation, it turned out that their chief credit officer's son was a chef and poured Lagunitas Pils in NYC, and his daughter's unlikely name was the same as my wife's: Carissa. Too weird, but it was apparently meant to be.

Even this happy ending has an interesting twist. Our new bank has since been caught up in the next crashing wave: commercial real-estate defaults. They are a very savvy bank and had no exposure to sub-prime business, but the problems have bled out and into their commercial real-estate tier lately. In late 2009 they accepted some of that Yuan-flavored TARP money and then later got a heavy-handed visit from the Federal Reserve and are now under the gun. They seem to be good and very smart people, and we sure wish them the best. Even as they work through their issues, they have remained very supportive of our business and were completely able to fund our "high-growth-case" capital equipment purchase requirement for 2010. So far so good!

Having said all of that, on the afternoon of the very day the news broke about their difficulties with the Federal Reserve regulators, two other very prominent (and so far solvent) California banks sent their loan folk over to visit us and share a beer in our Beer Sanctuary. One even took us to see a Warriors game in their luxury skybox. It was a very nice view! This has been a big change for desperate little Lagunitas. I think that as long as we keep our powder dry, we will have all the latitude we will ever need to continue growing as a strong and bankable entity. What a long, strange trip it's been.

Brown Shugga' Winter, 2008

There is a symmetry to everything. Hot will always cool. Up always comes to down. Markets rise and crash. $2 per gallon then $4 per gallon then $2. First the right begets the left; then the left becomes the right; and then the right becomes the wrong all over again. Hop prices do soar and then the just as surely crash and everyone cries except the brewer. Some drugs are legal (like alcohol) while others are forbidden. Some pleasures are embraced and are also forbidden. Ask the former NY Governor or PeeWee Herman. Saddam and Noreiga once got paychecks from the CIA. The King of Beers becomes another's mare. GM becomes Gee...Um... How many times have you heard an unusual word several times in one day. What is one day undercover- is the next day revealed- and then slunks back down where it came from again. The sun went down today and returns tomorrow as if for the first time. When governments are simple, people are simple. When governments are clever, people are clever. Earth mirrors heaven. There is a symmetry to everything.

Equinox Ale, Summer, 1997

Shall I compare thee to a summers day? Thou art more hoppy and more carbonate. Rough winds do not shake the darling buds of May, And summer's lease hath all too short a date: Sometimes too hot the eye of heaven shines, And often is your grieving thirst undimmed: And every fair from fair sometime declines, By chance, or natures changing course untrimmed: But thy eternal flavor shall not fade Nor lose possesion of that fair thou owest; Nor shall Thirst brag thou wanderest in his shade When in eternal lines to time thou growest. So long as men can breathe or eyes can see So long lives this, and this gives life to thee.

7

THE BIRTH OF A BRAND

A ROSE BY ANY OTHER NAME . . .

*N*inety-nine *times out of a hundred, when* we encounter something new, it doesn't turn out to be "new" after all. Most things have been around, at least gestating somewhere, for quite a while, figuring themselves out while deeply engaged in the invisible (and sometimes lengthy) process of becoming. I mean, who knew that the Lexus you drive today started as a company that built a really good textile loom? So it is that while, in 2014, the Lagunitas brand family is built around solid session beers and other adventurous big-beer flavors, it sure didn't start out that way. When I first set out on this trip in 1993, I wanted to do only local draft beers made twelve kegs at a time and hand-sold in the bars and restaurants of West Marin under their own individual names. I suppose I hoped that word would sneak out about this small brewer in the back of an old grocery store, but that was secondary. The idea of brewing only private labels was to secure the handles as best as I could, and I figured that if the venues could use their own name on my beers, they would stick around. I didn't know anything special about the craft-beer business, and what I did know about it sounded volatile and competitive.

At that time, retailers often switched beers on and off almost weekly as newer beers came to market, and newer brands were coming into the San Francisco market every day. I was still printing on the side, which involved more than a little traveling, so I needed to find a way to make the tap handles stick. I guess I engaged the self-interest of the good retailer. Interestingly, although the earliest private-label retail customers have all changed the handles over to Lagunitas-branded handles, 100 percent of our first accounts are still in place decades later. It's good to have friends!

The private labeling did have its limitations, and it did not travel well out of the tourist-intensive area and into beer bars in general. That really limited our opportunities, so the first actual Lagunitas-branded handle arrived in a cool, craft-centric bar in the East Bay. It got me to thinking. Later, when we were evicted from our first space by that cranky septic system and moved to an industrial area in Petaluma, I realized that we would need to be our own brand, and I had to start to think about what kind of brand we might want to be.

I quickly realized that I knew even less about brand building than I had about brewing or the business of beer, but that gave me a unique perch to innovate from. A good friend of mine from the printing times was a professional designer—not package labels and such, but brochures and catalogues. He was a very creative and quirky guy, and we had a good time developing the first two labels back in 2001: Dogtown Pale and Bug Town Stout. Even better, he did it for free!

As I said, I didn't really know anything about brand building, but I did know a lot about melody, thematic development, recapitulation, mutation, thematic variation, restatement, and so on—symphonic form. I decided I would just draw on my experiences in music to create our brand as a very long-form (Ten years? Twenty years?) symphony. We would reveal ourselves in the way of a seduction, learning about branding, our company, and ourselves at the same time.

Some products, whether a beer or a must-have Christmas toy, come to market very forcibly. They are imposed on you; you are dared not to appreciate them, dared to be the only one who doesn't have them, dared not to desire them. And in that process they take something from you as well. But craft brewing was born as an independent challenge to the status quo and appealed to people who saw themselves as individuals, people who thought for themselves. Since we would be speaking to these people, who were/are intuitive and intelligent, it seemed to me that a seduction was the only path with heart.

The challenge in any seduction, of course, is patience, and in business, patience takes money and time, of which we had neither. It's funny, though, if you are lucky enough to actually get a stolen mental fore-sighted peek down that "yet-to-be" corridor and see the path to your aspiration so clearly, the facts, time, and money (and the lack thereof) are nuisances and just get in the way.

The first Lagunitas brands were the Dogtown Pale Ale and the Bug Town Stout in twenty-two-ounce bombers. They were both names of extinct towns along Highway One in West Marin. I drove by those sites every couple of days while making my deliveries up and down One. The Bug Town had a big yellow and red bug on it, and the Dogtown had an attractive and ridiculous/noble dog head on it. The rest of the design was pretty much up to my designer friend's sense of form and color.

Beyond the names, I hadn't much time to live in the question of what we wanted to be as a brand. I only wanted to root the names in our West Marin home and for the labels to look Old West–meets–uptown San Francisco. In other words, to look like they'd been around for more than a little while. My friend and I wrote tongue-in-cheek copy on that first label, the beginning of an enduring tradition. On the Dogtown we wrote, "No dogs were harmed in the brewing pro-cess," and the Bug Town said, "Contains no actual insects." Not all that funny, but it was a start. The "No dogs were harmed" line has earned us a place in the hearts of the wacky and soulful PETA clan, and they have since had our beer at their annual fundraiser every year. These were the beginnings of the personality of our label and brand.

Our first bottling staff was all volunteers. Jason (later the head brewer), Coley, Lung Butter, Junior, Kona, Tenchy, Franz, Messy Jes-sie, and later a hundred others who would occasionally stop by after the word got out to the twenty-one-and-older skateboard set in Pet-aluma that if they put in a day at the brewery they'd get all the speed metal and Irish drinking songs they could stand, a free lunch, and short-filled bottles to take home. There was no shortage of takers, and they became our evangelist crew, telling crazy stories about the plant and helping the world get to know us from the inside out. We still buy lunch for the whole company every Friday in remembrance of things past. Every year I try to remember to tell some of these stories at our company Christmas party so that the new folks all know and everyone will remember that everything they take for granted at Lagunitas came from somewhere, from some chain of weird events, from some unseen person who came before them. It's a five-dimensional fractal web of directed causality.

By the way, we eventually realized that the economics of using volunteers and paying them in short-fills had a very Greenspanian flaw. I assumed that the crew would try to do a good job and be as efficient as they could be, and for a long time they did just that. But eventually they discovered interesting ways to rig the "outcomes," meaning the filled bottles that were put in cases on pallets to load onto trucks.

It went like this: the manual bottle filler was a neat little home-made home-brewer-on-steroids thing, and it relied on the craft of the human operator instead of gears and journals and cams and such. It only took a little while for one of the operators to realize that they could improve their take-home booty of short-filled bottles by "accidentally" creating more short-fills. I guess that is just human nature, Mr. Greenspan! For a while, things went on like that, and it was all cool, but as the booty stash got bigger and bigger, I noticed the volunteers loading dozens of cases of short-fills into their trunks and pickup beds at the end of the day. I started to worry.

Eventually, they made enough shorts to move the needle on our mostly insensitive efficiency meter. The short-fill numbers went through the roof, and sellable beer kinda dried up. I realized that it was time to get the crew on payroll, and so, one summer afternoon in 1996, we hired the best of the volunteers and had ourselves an actual bottling department for the first time ever. We already had a couple of the brewers on payroll, and with the bottling department, we suddenly had a fully staffed brewery. In a lot of ways it was a relief, because once you were really paying people, you could actually ask them to start at a certain time and work a certain way, and Lagunitas began to earn some money as a business.

But I have, well, you know, digressed.

Where were we? Yes, the entire exercise in branding was a process of elimination. If it worked, it stayed; if it didn't work, so long. The dog quickly gained fans, as did the beer. The stout and its accompanying bug were less successful, and while I would have liked the bug to succeed—just because no one puts bugs on labels—it didn't. We brewed the beer until 2002, and it was a nice beer, but I often wonder if the bug itself did it in. That question came up again years later while we were once again feeling around the fuzzy edges of what sort of casting against type we could achieve in the form of a delicious hoppy red ale called, simply, Ragwater. The name was purloined from a Tom Waits tune ("And you're so full of ragwater, bitters, and blue ruin that you're spillin' out over the side to anyone who'll listen"). It was a cool brew. But nobody ever knew if it was delicious or not, because the beer never even left the shelf. In 2007 I revived the recipe under a different name, and it did very nicely and earned good reviews. But not the Bug Town, and not the Ragwater. A rose by any other name might not really smell as sweet.

I spend a lot of time comparing recipes and labels to thematic development in a musical context. I spend less time thinking about the name and the label as a gimmick. They are partners. The label animates the brew, gives it a voice. But clearly it is *not* about the label in the end. I guess a turd by any other name *would* still smell as bad. It is an important lesson that we never have had a sucky recipe do well just because of a good name . . . and there *have* been some sucky recipes. Well, maybe just one. Maybe.

I can't really say that I ever had any idea what was going to work, but we'd try stuff this random way and see what happened. Something like walking down a long hallway, trying each door you pass. Some doors are locked, some open but there is nothing for you behind them. Maybe behind some are a couple dozen good folks, and behind others there are tens upon thousands of folks there just waiting for you to have knocked and invited yourself in. The Brown Shugga', the Zappa labels, and the Little Sumpin' releases worked like that. Maybe it is less a process of deciding than it is a process of elimination.

The dog, however, has persisted, and that little critter has even clawed its way off the label and back into the real world. New employees over the years, and brewery visitors as well, very casually bring their pooches to the brewery, certain that we must be a very dog-friendly culture. The good news is that we are, but that is a nice coincidence. When we opened up our Beer Sanctuary in the summer of 2010, folks automatically brought their dogs, proclaiming it "dog-friendly." It wasn't necessarily set up to be that way, but the dogs themselves made it so.

It is cool how much like a mirror a brand is, and that the things that people see in it can actually *become it* over time. I suppose that big breweries spend a lot of money on studies that tell them what people see in their brand so that they can do more of it, but down here, closer to the surface, it is easy to see it all firsthand. Stephen King wrote in *On Writing* about the emergence of completely unintended themes in his writing. He said that writing something, he'll go back and reread it to look for ideas that he didn't intend but that somehow rose up accidentally to add deeper meaning. Carl Jung put it another way: "The artist [the brand] is essentially the instrument, and he stands below his work, for which reason we should never expect from him an interpretation of his own work." These things are true and are just about the coolest things about originating a brand.

Brian Eno took it a step further, coaching to "Accept thy error as a secret intention." I dig that idea the most. An example with our labels would be spelling errors. Ore wrather, speling erorrs. For too long, I did not know that the design program I used had a spell-checker, and I am a miserable speller. So it happened that there was, and usually still is, a spelling error (or two) on just about every label. I receive e-mails every few weeks from someone who has taken the time to proofread a label. What could be cooler and more intimate? Sometimes I tell people that, just like the flaws purposefully woven into every Southwest American Indian rug, I intentionally place a spelling error in every label to avoid offending a flawless and possibly pompous God. It sounds convincing.

But I digress once again.

We began printing the labels and filling a pale and a stout in June, and by August we decided that we wanted to do a seasonal release, and with that, I had to make my first label on my own. After the creation of the first two labels with my friend, I realized that we were going to need lots and lots more design work, and I really felt like I'd pushed his generosity in getting the first two done, so I decided I had to learn to do labels myself. For some reason it did not seem too daunting. I would go to a Kinko's, where I could use Adobe Illustrator on their timed rental Macs. (First, though, I would go into the computer's system folder and turn off the rental timer clock. I'm still ashamed. Every dollar mattered back then.) I'd open my designer friend's original

Adobe Illustrator Dogtown Pale Ale label file and mess with it by clicking on and changing things until I got a basic understanding of what was what. Mostly I made up weird posters and table tents and tap handles and such.

The first label I did was for an Oktoberfest. I futzed with it until it looked a little like the pale and stout, only it was just black-and-white, and then I xeroxed it at Kinko's on cream-colored paper. I made up a weird little story about the previously unrecognized history of the origins of Oktoberfest:

> The original derivation of the word "Oktoberfest'" was actually the phrase, "Ach! Tuber Fest!" This antiquious expression refers back to the Dark Age reign of Sir Loin of Boef, during which there existed a brisk European trade in captured Irish slaves. The prevailing Germanic Lords imported Irishmen to work in their central European potato plantations. These Irish slaves were notorious for their endurance in drinking festivals under the new moon and during the potato harvest. They would brew up huge batches of a unique fermented alcoholic potato beer. The Irishmen eventually introduced their German masters to this unusual beer-like beverage. The harvest parties centered around this brew, hence the term 'Tuber-fest." The slaves were finally freed during the European potato blights of 1252 and 1257. Years later malted barley was substituted for the spuds of old and, well, the rest is history. Honest . . .

We got a bunch of confused "Is that the truth?"–type calls at the brewery, so I figured that we were onto something.

When it came to the second seasonal, everybody wanted to have a swing at making a recipe, and a lot of guys all became brewmasters at once. There were lots of complications. My soon-to-be-former brewer demanded that we do a fruit beer. Ick.

Once, we did a Peach Wheat Ale (but the flavoring was actually apricot; I don't remember why). The beer was weird and the label was terrible, with a story that doesn't even bear reprinting here.

But we were on our way. The next would be a brew to celebrate our one-hundredth batch. It would become our IPA.

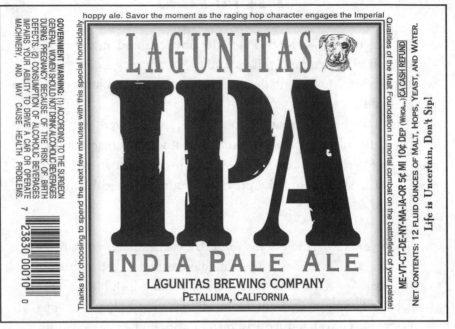

Thanks for choosing to spend the next few minutes with this special homicidially hoppy ale. Savor the moment as the raging hop character engages the Imperial Qualities of the Malt Foundation in mortal combat on the battlefield of your palate!

LAGUNITAS

IPA

INDIA PALE ALE

LAGUNITAS BREWING COMPANY
PETALUMA, CALIFORNIA

ME-VT-CT-DE-NY-MA-IA-OR 5¢ MI 10¢ DEP (WHOA...) CA CASH REFUND

NET CONTENTS: 12 FLUID OUNCES OF MALT, HOPS, YEAST, AND WATER.

Life is Uncertain, Don't Sip!

First Brewed in September, 1994

"Here, have a beer. It will make you right." Ernest said to Tarzan. Tarzan had never had the true beer before and Ernest knew this would not be his last. He drank the beer quickly. It was cold, and Tarzan knew this too. He looked at the beer coolly. "Me Tarzan, you beer." Ernest looked at Tarzan and felt old. "Vas iz schviss vit da old schtuff?" Ernest and Tarzan turned to watch as Sigmund entered the room strangely. "Sigmund," Ernest said, "my old primitivo! Have a beer with us". Sigmund knew what Ernest meant and he could not bear it. They all had a beer, and it was good. Ernest said "Do you remember how it was in Stinson with the running of the dogs and how we ate crullers and got drunk on the Lagunitas Pale and stole the grunion from the young girls at the Cafe de Sand Shekel?" Sigmund thought of how Ernest could be cruel and he did not answer. He thought how only dogs were not cruel. And also how sometimes a cold beer was just a beer. Tarzan thought of nothing. They all ordered contuuzti del corratzo and spoke not of their big cigars.

8

THE ARRIVAL OF OUR IPA

Robert Frost should have said, "We were the land's before the land was ours." Lagunitas IPA was brewed the first time flawlessly, and we have strived ever after to keep it the same while we replaced every piece of equipment over the years. I wrote the recipe, but it was directly inspired by the very best brewer in the North Bay, who brewed the most sophisticated and subtle beers in the very tiniest and most compact brewery I'd ever seen: Calistoga Brewing Co.

Developing recipes now is a pretty straightforward business because there are so many brewers and so many other breweries. Our collective vocabulary of flavors is pretty huge. Back in the early 1990s, though, it was pretty much a lot of experimentation and guesswork, and most people who were into craft brewing did not come from brewing schools—at least not the people I knew. There were and are still only four basic ingredients in beer: malted barley, hops, yeast, and water. Of course, now there are barrel flavors and bacteria flavors and seed flavors and all sorts of cool inputs. But in the early 1990s, craft beer was still such a unique idea that just using the basic four ingredients well was a revelation to the taste buds of the world. There are gobs of different varieties of each of those four things, and that scope generates the incredible range of recipe flavors that exist.

Our water came to us as is. Our barley malt came pre-milled. But I could use any hops I wanted, and at first I just picked yeast strains at random. In 1993 and 1994 I was working with a yeast I'd had some success with while home-brewing, but I'd never been satisfied with the results once I was making beer on even the smallest of commercial scales. Even late into 1994 I was really frustrated with the beer I was making, and I was constantly modifying the recipes to try to bring out the flavors I had in my mind. The yeast was this damned Altbier strain, and the beer it made tasted like, well, nothing. I didn't really realize at the time to what degree the other ingredients and processes were secondary to the yeast with respect to flavor. In its country of origin, this yeast may have been loved for the "clean" flavor it produced, but to me, in brash craft-brewing America, it tasted like nothing. I tried adding small amounts of various specialty malts and lots of different hops at many and varying times in the kettle—late hopping, dry hopping, pre-hopping, uber-hopping, everything I could think of. The recipe became increasingly complex and detailed, and the beer continued to taste like nothing.

Then one perfect summer Sunday afternoon, my wife and I were at my now-friend Randy Gremp's pub in Calistoga, sitting in its beer garden deep in wine country. We were nibbling on jalapeno-lime crab cakes and savoring Randy's delicious ESB and a delicate pilsner, as the whole world dissolved into one with the sky and the trees and the creek and the vines and the day and the beer. I was so knocked out by Randy's flavors, and I was so at wit's end with my own recipes, that I decided to get up all my courage. Later that week, I called him on the phone and asked him a question that I was sure he would view as intrusive: "What yeast strain do you use?" I was very nervous when I called and introduced myself and asked the question.

The words almost caught in my throat, but to my surprise, he straight-out just told me. That was a completely unforeseen generosity. I have the very worst imaginable short-term memory, especially for numbers, which is how yeast strains are most often designated. Even as I hung up the phone, blown away that the question was well received and excited by the simple fact that he'd share his secret with me, I realized that I was well into the process of forgetting the number. I quickly retrieved the "sounds" of the numbers from my memory, the way most people remember a melody, and scribbled them onto my hand with a Sharpie, and then right onto my desktop for safety. I called up our yeast supplier and ordered the yeast immediately. Maybe this all sounds a little pathetic, and you think I should have been a more diligent brewer and found my own solution, but this is the thing: I was too busy. I had a bunch of employees, a few distributors, I was still working some in the brewery, I had another job, I had a wife, I was running out of money, and I didn't like my own beer. I guess I was a little like Ted Turner cutting across the coral reef because of a bad start. It was desperate, and it worked.

So I ordered the yeast, and when it arrived, we brewed up a batch of our pale ale with it, and the hidden flavors—all of the different malts and hops added at all those different times—leapt out of the glass at us in an explosion of something new in beer. That was the batch that was scheduled to be our first bottled release under the newborn Lagunitas Dogtown Pale Ale label.

At that time, bottling brewers didn't really use a lot of different ingredients in every recipe, and hopping was mostly focused into the first addition (at the start of the boil) with some smaller additions at the very end or in the whirlpool for aromatic purposes—not those big middle and late additions of high alpha hops that are so common now. Malts were somewhat more varied, but each recipe was mostly built on just a few. A handful of good and adventurous brewpubs made exceptions to this.

The recipes of the bottling brewers who were well established in the market at that time were structured the way they were because those recipes sprang from home-brewing, and home-brewing was still mostly about trying to re-create the historic traditions of European beers of the 1500s and 1600s. It was a noble pursuit! The way the whole Western world dug out from the Dark Ages was to look back a few centuries to Greek and Roman aesthetics in order to build upon and find new ideals that spoke to their new world. The origins of craft brewing weren't much different. The beer world of the 1960s and 1970s was very similar to the Dark Ages—but without the plague. Those archetypal European recipes were built on the malting technology of the day, which was pretty rustic. (Hell, the thermometer wasn't even invented as a useful industrial control until 1760!) Hop varieties were limited and probably pretty scarce too. Still, as straightforward as the first microbrews were—pale ales, ambers, goldens, ESBs, reds, wheats, porters, and stouts—they were a revelation, and although they changed everything, they were pretty simple compared to where things have gotten to today.

It was the 1994 world that we began bottling into. For Lagunitas to find a place out there, I had to create a unique selling proposition, and I liked my stronger home brews. Because of our rough teacher in the form of our old Altbier yeast, we'd just plain loaded all the complexity possible into the mash tun, and then even more into the kettle. With that change of yeast and the unexpected results, I saw our recipe structure come forever into focus.

I've read some smarty-pants one-line beer reviews complaining that Lagunitas beers all have a similar flavor profile. This familiar flavor flows from our yeast strain. It is a great flavor: malty while still allowing for pretty heavy hopping without burying the malt backbone in the brew. So, right they are. But isn't it a little cool that you can always recognize a Rolling Stones song too?

Working with the new yeast was a revelation, and the next recipe brewed with it was the third seasonal release, Lagunitas IPA. The tiny first kettle hop addition and the very late giant kettle hopping we had developed were new concepts in bottled beers in 1994. My favorite pub brewer, Grant Johnston at Marin Brewing Co., was the only other one doing this that I knew of, and his beers were magnificent. The packaging breweries were still mostly emulating those European styles, and higher alcohol and higher hop rates like ours were just not being bottled. It was all those ESBs, pale ales, steams, amber ales, golden ales, pilsners, marzens, red ales, porters, wheat beers (honeyed, fruited, unfruited, unfiltered, whatevered). Sour beers did sometimes occur, but no one drank them on purpose! In that way, at that time in the world of West Coast craft brewing, I believe that we (and another quiet but great brewer out of Newport, Oregon) played the biggest role in getting the future Big Beer Train on its tracks.

The industry was also plowing through a rough time, and making special beers was the most important element to fuel my brewery's unfettered growth. During this period, circa 1996 to 1999, the industry was mired in the sucky part of the "business cycle," as it's known in MBA circles. Through that entire period, beginning when one thousand new breweries opened, through 2000, Lagunitas grew at a rate that was way exciting—as well as the exception. In seventeen years, our growth has always exceeded 22 percent.

Each year, when the late 1990s annual craft-industry overview was published in the *New Brewer* magazine, complete with a ranking and growth scorecard, we were often the fastest-growing brewery in percentage terms, and always among the four or five fastest-growing in terms of raw barrel growth, year in and year out. Lots of the brewing class of the 1980s was either staggering in place, stumbling backward, or dying altogether. That went on for four or five years. But through all of it we, while small, grew and did so quietly and quickly. I'm sure that drew the attention of new entrants who were looking to be in a faster-moving part of the stream. The things we were doing worked in our market, and that informed the plans of the new brewers of the time. The prevailing winds on the continent have always blown from west to east, and beer culture is no exception. From grunge to surf-speak to craft beer, the news is carried on these westward-originating winds. As word spread eastward, the breweries in those regions started making "West Coast style" ales too. The whole thing was off and running. Eventually, the easterners took the "West Coast style" label off their beer descriptions and made it their own by doing it their own way. The flavors were resinous and meaty rather than just malty or bitter, with way-higher-than-ordinary IBUs (international bittering units) going in the kettle.

But, for a change, allow me to digress.

Sometimes it's a little distressing how even the short history of our little industry is lost as new players enter the field, respecting nothing, and certain that they were born perfect incarnations of craft-brewing prowess, not the least bit cognizant of the breweries that came before them and that laid the roadway that they so easily drive on, burning rubber where they will. Lagunitas derived its identity from the industry that we entered as well as from our own sources. We came out of something special, and our influences are things we are proud of. I have cited my true hero brewers every year on our Lucky 13 label, and until recently I had never seen that sort of thing done by any other beer company.

When we bought the bones of the closed Napa Ale Works brewery I did a special twenty-two-ounce label to recognize the passing of a great. It was sad to be part of taking someone's dream down and loading it onto a truck. I read once where one particularly pious brewer described the troubles of the late 1990s as a form of justice, and suggested that those brewers who failed just weren't good businessmen—which I assume he was certain that he himself was. That was pretty thoughtless talk. There is no recognition of what has been lost when something dies. People who built the industry that I began inhabiting in 1993 leveraged everything to get into it. They borrowed (and sometimes lost) on their homes, cars, marriages, reputations, and other careers. Now that craft brewing is past its infancy and its potential is more easily accessed, there is (like our sister industry, fine wine) lots of less accountable money—vanity money, mostly—flowing into craft, and like it does in fine wine, money distorts and usurps things. This is how business works, I guess, but it is perceptibly less soulful. We are in good shape now as a company, and will stay that way going forward, and I'm proud of our funky upbringing, so I don't write this as sour grapes. It's just that lack of modesty rubs me the wrong way. To you I say: Ye faire consumer: know your brewer. Drink the work of people you personally relate to and have a reason to trust and want to support. Why not? You do become what you drink.

Conventional style versus innovation is a theme that has dogged us over the years. We used to send our IPA to the Great American Beer Festival every year. We were always judged poorly. The comment sheets that were returned to us in the 1990s would uniformly say things like "Too bitter for style, but an excellent product." Later, the comments morphed into "Not strong enough, not bitter enough for the style, but an excellent product." Whatever. I have never been very interested in winning contests. Even if Lagunitas were to win, say, a bronze medal (which, hey, we did, actually) for the Pils in a European beer contest (where the world's best lagers are made), we would never put that on the label. Beer speaks (for itself).

Over the years, the IPA label has changed a lot, and at the same time, not at all. I think of it as more clearly becoming itself. When the label first came to be on the Kinko's Mac at 5:00 AM one fall morning in 1995, it seemed to be born, not created—the way sculptors talk about their work being a process of revealing a form that already existed within the marble. As my minor design skills have improved, I have been better able to help its elemental self escape its constraints. It is as if it always existed and was just waiting to be found, but, of course, I'm the proud father. If you check out www.BeerLabels.com, you can see almost every single incarnation of our label, as well as many others.

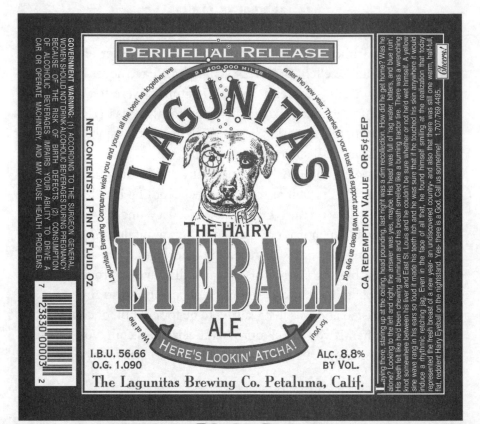

NET CONTENTS: 1 PINT 6 FLUID OZ

7 23850 00003 2

PERIHELIAL RELEASE

91,400,000 MILES

Lagunitas Brewing Company and you wish you and yours all the best as together we enter the new year. Thanks for your trust and support. We'll keep an eye out for you! We at the

LAGUNITAS

THE HAIRY

EYEBALL

ALE

HERE'S LOOKIN' ATCHA!

I.B.U. 56.66
O.G. 1.090

ALC. 8.8%
BY VOL.

The Lagunitas Brewing Co. Petaluma, Calif.

CA REDEMPTION VALUE OR-5¢ DEP

Cheers!

Laying there, staring up at the ceiling, head pounding, last night was a dim recollection. How did he get home? Was he alone? Looking to the left and right, the answer was yes, maybe. His head was full of 'rag water, bitters, and blue misery'. His teeth felt like he'd been chewing aluminum and his breath smelled like a burning tractor tire. There was a wrenching knot somewhere between his liver and East St. Louis and he couldn't be sure whether or not he'd wet himself. A yellow sine wave rang in his ears so loud it made his teeth itch and he was sure that if he touched his skin anywhere it would induce a rhythmic retching jag. Even in the face of all that, he found himself smiling at the realization that today represented the fresh breast of a new year- an undiscovered country- and also that there was still one warm, half-full, flat, redolent Hairy Eyeball on the nightstand. Yes- there is a God. Call us sometime! 1.707.769.4495.

LAYING THERE, staring up at the ceiling, head pounding, last night was a dim recollection. How did he get home? Was he alone? Looking to the left and right, the answer was yes, maybe. His head was full of 'rag water, bitters, and blue misery'*. His teeth felt like he'd been chewing aluminum and his breath smelled like a burning tractor tire. There was a wrenching knot somewhere between his liver and East St. Louis and he couldn't be sure whether or not he'd wet himself. A yellow sine wave rang in his ears so loud it made his teeth itch and he was sure that if he touched his skin anywhere it would induce a rhythmic wretching jag. If all that weren't bad enough, he found himself smiling at the realization that there was still one warm, half-empty, flat, Hairy Eyeball on the nightstand. Ahhh- There is a God.

9

FLAVORS AND LABELS

*W*hen we began bottling, only the Dogtown and Bug Town twenty-two-ounce bottle labels were conventionally printed on nice shiny paper: Simpson C1S (coated on one side). This might as well have been the official paper of craft brewing, and everyone used it. All our later releases and seasonal products were all xeroxed at Kinko's on plain uncoated paper. This was because I never knew how much we were going to make of any one brew, and even though I had spent the previous eleven years of my life handling hundreds of printing orders for millions upon millions of pieces, for some reason I could not bring myself to commit to even a small printing order for my own business. Looking back, I have no idea why, but I clutched tightly to the idea that the crummy paper labels generated a sort of dynamic tension. It was like Sergio Leone casting Henry Fonda as a bad guy—there's tension from the first scene. It would be a great (I thought) beer in a crummy package. In truth, I remember looking across a bar at a Maker's Mark label and noticing that the high-quality, well-positioned whiskey was somehow granted a form of dignity by its plain paper label. Anchor Brewing's look had the same aesthetic at work. It seemed like good company. Soon thereafter, when Jim Beam rolled out the Knob Creek, Basil Hayden's, and Booker Noe lines, they all shared that same simple aesthetic that we employed for Lagunitas.

At the same time, the disposability of the label art allowed me to do a lot of fiddling to work up a look and feel that felt like beer, somehow told people something about us, and was also visible from the parking lot outside a liquor store. Sometimes I would stand in front of a beer cooler in a store and not be able to find the more conventional Dogtown Pale Ale or Bug Town Stout bottles on the shelf right at eye level, and that scared the heck out of me.

When I started working on the art for the then-seasonal Peach Wheat and later the Lagunitas IPA, I decided that it would have a look and feel different from the existing conventional labels. I suppose the look would *have* to have been different because, as I wrote earlier, I had no idea what I was doing! The first labels that I did with my designer friend had color and a picture and flowing shapes and stuff. All I had really figured out how to do on my own in a design program was to make boxes and set type, so that's what the labels still mostly are, and it works. Also, in this media world where the medium *is* the message, the words become the art. When you don't know what you are doing, anything is possible.

But this complete divergence from the Dog and Bug labels would also be the seed for a second and higher-priced line of beers. We were not making any money with the Dogtown and Bug Town priced so low, even though that was where the craft-beer market was at that point. The newer beers would have a bigger flavor profile, be stronger in general, and they'd have the plain-Jane (read: amateur-designed) label. I felt like we needed to raise prices, and that was a way to do it without changing anything that was already in place. From a brand-family structure standpoint, that was a key moment. The structure that we have evolved for our brand family has now evolved into an industry standard.

Our distributors all got very upset about the split pricing, and we were told that retailers would line-price both labels at the higher level, and that there was nothing we could do about it, but it didn't happen that way, and retailers were very fair with us. When we rolled out our six-packs later, we kept offering our twenty-two-ounce bombers as well. I'd thought about ending the twenty-two-ounce version of the brews we were planning to sell as six-packs, but my marketing director talked me into keeping them all going. That turned out to be huge for us. Many of our contemporaries stopped doing twenty-twos when they rolled out six-packs.

Keeping them going turned out to be a great decision for Lagunitas, and for many years it was only us and our local brewpubs still doing twenty-twos. Compare that to today's beer shelf! The bombers were and are a great way to do experimental brews and learn a lot along the way. Today, it seems every brewery is back to doing twenty-twos, and while it has become a lot more crowded on the shelf, it is great for consumers and gives everyone a chance to try out new stuff. I don't know if our modest success through the difficult mid-1990s caught the eyes of other brewers or if it was just the logical way to do it, but it is the way it is done now. Just recently even the phlegmatic capital-*B* brands have begun to rejigger their lineups in this mold. In hindsight, it kinda makes ya feel cool to have been out front.

But I digress.

Once the IPA label was done and the beer was in the bottle, the die was cast and our brand's method of communicating was set. The look was established by what I could not do with the design, and that was being fancy. I have a strong feel for positive and negative space in design, and I'm comfortable arranging type elements. There was descriptive text on the side, and the paper was uncoated. I employed three or four basic typefaces, and everything flowed from there. By making a few simple rules for myself, a brand was born. Everything comes from somewhere, and the IPA label was no exception.

The feel was Maker's Mark, the information and recipe disclosure was inspired by the great Rogue Ales, and the writing concept really came from the original J. Peterman catalogs. That was a long time before *Seinfeld* made such a joke out of the J. Peterman character. The catalogs had a short blurb alongside each clothing item, but it was not descriptive; rather, the clothing item was an element in a larger narrative. It was not what the jacket actually looked like, but instead the simple fact that it was draped neatly, but forgotten, over a chair in a dimly lit café on a narrow street in Tangiers, while its owner was busy in the next room negotiating for the release of a band of Hutu tribes-men who were providing intelligence to the MI5 and had recently been taken hostage in Sudan, although no ransom amount had yet been established. (Yes, I just made that all up. I don't know anything about Hutus or ransom. But it's fun.)

The idea was the romance, not just the product. Most other brew-eries at the time were engaged in dead-end wine talk about perfect balances and subtle blends of this and that, and tawny hues and floral noses and boring, boring, boring. And did I mention boring? I wanted to go a lot further and speak to our consumers as if they were intelli-gent, get closer to them, and have a good time treating the product a little more lightly. After all, it is just beer. Special beer? Yes, but that is why I took so much time writing carefully.

Designing a label from scratch is a rush. If you're thinking about starting up your own thing, by all means, do your own design work, even if you have a more skilled designer help you finish it for produc-tion. By doing the design yourself, you will learn a lot about what you are selling, who you are talking to, and how you want to be under-stood by the world. It is a deep test of your own vision for your com-pany and a deeper test of your willingness to learn new things starting from zero, and that will be a very routine occurrence, especially if your enterprise grows, and learning it yourself is way, way cheaper. I'd had a year vaguely studying design at a great school on the near South Side of Chicago, but that was no credential for doing the full deal like I found myself having to do. Design was fun, but just the work of writ-ing a side label on a beer bottle was crazy and engaging.

I had no background as a writer either, but I knew I had a point of view, and that is what you want your potential customers to under-stand. It is what makes you different from any of your peers. If you don't have a point of view, a vision, a personality, then you oughta work on that for a while first.

For me, more often than not, a copywriting session went some-thing like this: 4:30 AM at Kinko's, hands to the keyboard, the blank canvas, first a word (let's start with *sometimes*), and then it would

begin—"Sometimes, when she [a character appears] would walk backwards with the small balding bird on her shoulder [WTF?] reminding her of her days spent rebuilding the malt mill [a brewing term
injected] back in Ashtabula [a pointless Dylan reference] it seemed as
though all the world was a cold beer [close a circle]." And so the story
would reveal itself. It became a trip to see how the story would end
without personally interfering with it. In the best case, it was almost
like taking dictation. Beer was always a magnetic pole in the story, and
sometimes it would seem too easy, but then I would remind myself
that it *was* a story on a beer bottle, and it seemed natural.

More than once I resisted the attractive power of the subject of
beer, and the story would seem to hover above the label, not really
attached to it, in a way that was interesting. On those labels I would
end the story with something like "And what does this all have to do
with beer?" The hard work in the writing was brevity and compression.
The space is constrained. If you write expansively, you get a novel, but
compression yields poetry—if you are very, very lucky. I always hoped
to get lucky. There is a slashing of adjectives, removal of unnecessary
articles, elimination of puffery, and deleting of pronouns. Sometimes,
though, you just get uncontrollable run-on sentences. It is amazing
how much of what you write you can cut without losing any of the
intent, and if you're lucky it can become more powerful. I'd guess that
is true about most of our conversations too. Do people idly chatting at
a bar ever sound like birds chirping to you?

I am proud that the brewery's founder (me) wrote (and still does)
all the recipes while also designing and producing all the labels. That
is important, and I think it is also uncommon. A brewery can hire
out those functions and guide them with an intimate hand, but there
is always a gap between the vision and the execution, and there are
committee-like inputs and compromises that enter the formula. It
can't be helped. That is why I recommend you do the design and writing yourself. You might like Aerosmith's recent albums, but they don't
write all their own stuff anymore, and you can hear it. Their new songs
lack the immediacy of their early inspiration. A singer-songwriter

either sinks or swims. For us: so far so good. When one apprehends the Lagunitas brand, there is a point source—a core personality—and I hope that comes through in the form of a vibe.

In my former life (and in my experience, every brewer has a former life), I studied music composition, and the structure of that world is reflected in the way our brand emerges. One person sits alone and quietly conceives a musical work, beginning with a fragment of an idea (similar to a beer flavor). Then the real work begins, to bring it out of the ether and encode it in graphic form on paper by scribbling a bunch of dots onto a bunch of lines (this is the recipe and label). The finished idea is released to real live musicians (brewers and label printers), who bring their own unique process to the graphically represented work's realization in the form of a performance (brewing and printing labels). The final piece may be recorded, and if it is, it can be reproduced into infinity (the bottling line).

The first label to really take flight with its side story was that Oktoberfest label back in 1995. It seemed funny at the time. But the idea that took root in my mind was that reality was negotiable and that the bottle could be its own parallel funhouse mirror, with its own rules and accountabilities. It became a canvas and was no longer just a container. Other breweries that opened in the years after us have used this idea and taken it in their own directions. Plagiarism really is the highest form of imitation, and as another quasi-peer once informed me, "You can't trademark the alphabet."

Right you are.

The main thing was to get as much of our genuine personality onto the label as possible. Since I started the brewery, and since I did the design, I suppose the personality I was mining was my own, but the labels never were "me." I'm not really that interesting. In fact, when visitors come to the brewery, a common question is, "Who writes all that stuff on the labels?" When we are introduced, I can always sense the subtle disappointment, but I am not bummed out about that. I'm a middle-class suburban white guy from Nowheresville, Illinois, and there is something cool about having a more interesting alter ego. Like the real artists out there, I can be anything when I create a recipe and label, and there is a secret freedom in this truth. I've written things that were actually funny and sometimes uncomfortable, and I've written things that tried to say something important that I wanted to say but that the real me could never say with a straight face. I've gotten to publish imitation Hemingway, Pynchon, and Faulkner and impersonated Robert Parker and Ray Bradbury. I've plagiarized Woody Allen, Steve Martin, Emily Dickinson, Wallace Stevens, Yosemite Sam, Richard Feynman, and even Ben Franklin and Shakespeare. What could be more fun? I think that on a couple of occasions I may have even written a little Magee, but I can't be sure. Probably not.

After the Oktoberfest in 1995, we made our first holiday brew. Personally, I am not a big Christmas guy, although, thankfully, my wife is. I really didn't want to do a holiday label with snow and pine trees and gifts and all of that. I wanted to do something reflective of the season's darkness. The beer name came from a friend of the brewery who was a big Arnold fan. The first *Terminator* movie still held sway over our imaginations, and building on the traditional celebrator idea, he suggested we call it the Lagunator Ale. The beer was a big-for-the-time brown ale at 7.5 percent, and it got a lot of attention for being stronger. The recipe's success presaged January's coming Hairy Eyeball Ale at a whopping 9.2 percent.

The story on the Lagunator Ale label involved a brewer materializing between parked trucks on Christmas day and ended with "come with me if you want to live." The dog on the label sported wraparound shades, and the beer was as dark as the season. That too was something new in the craft-beer world. Conventional wisdom for holiday releases did not generally include the kinds of things we put on our promo materials about that beer: "We brewed this Special Ale to celebrate the darkness and depression that mar the holiday landscape." I don't know if it was a good idea or not, but the beer sold very well, and in the absence of e-mails from the world saying that we suck, I wondered if we'd said something that people recognized as authentic. I was emboldened. As a writer hero of mine, Jack Kerouac, once wrote,

"I want to fish as deep down as possible into my own subconscious in the belief that once that far down, everyone will understand because they are the same that far down."

As I mentioned, for a January seasonal release (and by the way, January seasonals were also not usually done at the time), we brewed a seriously strong brown ale. I wanted to name it the Eye of the Dog as an homage to a neighbor brewery to the north of which I was a genuine fan. But at the last minute we decided that they might not think it was so flattering, so another name was needed. I decided that a hangover cure was what the brew really was, so it was christened the Hairy Eyeball. It was a souped-up version of the Lagunator. The story on the side was a detailed description of the worst hangover ever, and ended with a ray of hope when the subject discovered that there is "still one half-empty, flat, warm Hairy Eyeball Ale left on the nightstand." Later years' releases of the Hairy Eyeball included a trilogy of a romance between an eyeball in a martini and a hairball on a bar top. Nobody knows why.

We followed that in March with the Eye of the Hairball Ale, a wheat-wine-styled thing. It was confusing for retailers and consumers. First the big dark hairy eyeball on the label and the confusing name change to a pale, pale, pale wheat wine. I got a message one night that went something like, "Uh, last night I was, like, having a Hairy Eyeball and it was great, and now tonight I'm, like, having an Eye of the Hairball, and, uh, I just want to know, what's going on?" I knew we were onto something good.

So where to go from there for a spring seasonal? The first name that appeared in my mind was Hair of the Dog Ball, but that lasted about two minutes before the female office contingent united in opposition. It really is a good thing to have a woman's touch in the office. The beer was a steroidal version of our IPA, so we came up with the name Maximus IPA. Although another brewer is somehow credited with inventing the double IPA (which is sorta like being credited with inventing the moon just by being the first to point at it), it is very likely that the Maximus and another cool brewer's IPA are truly the oldest continuously produced double IPAs in the great US of A, but

WTF does that mean? Nothing. It is about participating in the curve of history and staying excited about what you might do next, and that's about it.

The Maximus IPA label featured a Robert Parker–style run-on sentence involving an unnamed character borrowed from the Firesign Theatre work. A common fan sent the reference to the founder of the original Firesign, and all was very good. I later got to talk with this Firesign founder when I wanted to quote them ("We're all just bozos on this bus") on the 2009 Correction Ale. He was a very cool guy. All he asked was a trade of our wares with the label in consideration for the use. That was a joy to fulfill. I have worked with others who were very clinging and unfriendly about intellectual property, but I think that the Firesign guys know that their own well runs very deep, and they're not worried about having their work wander off the reservation from time to time. Handshakes among honest people are a powerful form of juju.

In the summer of 1996 I produced a recipe for a strange but popular pale oat ale called Equinox Ale. It was also something different. It was essentially an 8 percent oatmeal stout without any of the dark malts. It was also strong, not common at that time—especially for a summer release, which was usually when brewers would present lighter beers. But it struck a chord in that it followed no beer style rules and delivered a good value in its essential strength.

That same year, we also brought back the third recipe from the early private label days, the Cappuccino Stout. We have brewed that recipe every year since, without exception. Tasty, it is. The Cappuccino Stout was always a great recipe, and it was a good idea to put it in a bottle with its own label. The story on the side was an adaptation of the twenty-third Psalm: "Coffee is my shepherd, I shall not want." I expected that to draw some sort of criticism, but . . . nothin'. I guess God loves coffee too. Just recently, though, the TTB (the Alcohol and Tobacco Tax and Trade Bureau) told me that I had to change some of the story language that suggested to them that the coffee might wake you up: "Thou preparest a carafe for me in the presence of my zzz's." OK, whatever.

That winter led, naturally, to the Olde GnarlyWine release, which the following year was accidentally-on-purpose misbrewed into Brown Shugga' when a flock of one-pound C&H brown sugar boxes found their way into the kettle following my incorrect specification of the malt bill. The true story is that I screwed up the tiny bit of math necessary to write up the recipe sheet for the brewers, and at about 6:30 that night they called to tell me that something was wrong. After a little bit, the mistake became clear, so I asked them if they'd already added the bittering hops, which they had. Our bittering hop then was the now-extinct Eroica, which does not have a very nice flavor and was usually best to use only in the boiled-down first addition. I knew we needed to get the gravity up to put a little balance back into the deal— either that or just throw the brew out and start up fresh on Monday morning.

I decided to throw good money after bad, and asked the brewers to go to all the grocery stores in town and buy up all the brown sugar they could. Well, they did. Monday morning, I came into the brew house early and found two hundred empty one-pound C&H Golden Brown Sugar boxes scattered all over the floor. The batch was in a fermenter doing its business. I took a sample of the young brew, and it tasted like moldy ass. I felt stupid for making it worse, but we decided we would let it go and see what would happen. We tasted it every day and it stayed terrible, then got a little worse, and then suddenly, on day fifteen—as it has every year since then—it took on a sort of bourbon note with the candy flavors crisp and clear, and it was strong. The body was light, but it did not betray the actual strength of the brew.

In the years since, we've gotten used to late-night holiday phone messages that always start out like this: "Uh, last night we were, uh, drinking your Brown Shugga', and, uh, well, the weirdest thing happened . . ." I even have a Brown Shugga' story of my own. At a brewery function, after two quick pints of the stuff, I remember punching, being punched, feeling my arm twisting up behind my back, seeing the street outside rushing up toward me, and then waking up a hundred miles north at a rest stop on Highway 101 outside the town of Garberville with a sine wave parting my hair and no eyeglasses.

Life at the brewery wasn't all drunken hijinks, however. In 1997 we lost an employee the hard way. He was a young Samoan guy from a very traditional family, a big fellow named Junior. He had a heart of gold and very scary voices in his head. Too much so for his own peace of mind in the end. When he first came to the brewery to work on the bottling line, he was extremely quiet and private, and that made him seem a little intimidating. Nothing could have been further from the truth, and as he settled into the scene, he gradually opened up to us all. He would smile the purest sort of smile, and it was as if he'd found the first place where he felt accepted, and that was very cool to see.

But there was an arc to our experience of Junior, a steep personal parabola. One early winter Friday night he came back to the brewery as John, the night-shift brewer—a slight guy with an education as a physicist—was finishing up. Junior asked John some questions that completely unnerved him, so John told him he was done and needed to lock up. He did so quickly and got out of there. On Monday mornings, Junior usually came in to set up the bottling room, blaring "Iron Man" as he attached hoses and mixed sanitizer solutions. But the next Monday, he didn't show up. The bottling manager called his home, and we learned that he'd called a friend later that same Friday night and told him that he'd been hearing voices in his head that were telling him to hurt certain people. He'd said he knew that the voices were wrong but didn't know what to do about it, so he drank a quart of whiskey and ate a bunch of pills. It was a truly tragic story, and painful to lose a member of the Lagunitas family. One of the things that comes as a surprise in leading a business is how deeply you sometimes end up experiencing other people's inner lives. That was the deep end of the pool.

That year, 1997, we had thirty barrels of our holiday beer, the Lagunator Ale, left over that had been ready too late in the holiday season. I was worried that we would still be shipping holiday brew in January. So, as a memorial release, we took those thirty barrels and froze the brew three times in a bottling tank, each time transferring the unfrozen part of the batch to another tank and freezing it again, until we'd reduced it down to about ten barrels. The beer that emerged was like nothing else. It was like double cream, a deep brown/black, not very intensely bitter, and 18 percent alcohol (because freezing separates the water from the beer while leaving 96 percent of the alcohol and flavor constituents behind in a progressively smaller volume of liquid). We called it Big Junior Ale, and it was a great thing.

We have since brought back Big Junior on a couple of occasions: for Y2K and for our three-thousandth brew (B3K), and we are looking forward to bringing Junior back again in the future.

Around the same time, we also made a unique, never-to-be-repeated-on-Earth beer entirely from Eroica hops. They had been our first-addition kettle hop since I began home-brewing. I chose Eroica then *not* for its particular brewing qualities, but because it bore the name of a favorite Beethoven symphony. The Eroica hops were cool and spicy, even pine-tar flavored, sort of hoppy, and they added something interesting to our beer. One day I got a call from the hop dealer telling me that the farmer had grubbed the last acre of Eroica growing anywhere, so the six boxes he had left would be the last. I bought them all and made a beer eponymously named Eroica Ale. It was an extinction ale. Maybe another first? The label story ended with this sentence: "Drinking this rare ale is like standing in front of the cage of the last living animal of an endangered species, watching it die, and then eating it. Cheers!"

Speaking of which, our xeroxing of the labels allowed me to do small things within larger label runs. One sad fall day our family dog, the seventeen-year-old beloved Blue, passed on. I adapted a wood carving of Blue done by his original owner and substituted it for the regular label dog on the Oktoberfest release that was headed for the bottling line. I also wrote a label story while sitting on our deck in the unbearable hours after we got home from that last sad trip to our vet (also a shareholder now, by the way). I made up about a thousand of those special labels, and we put one bottle with that label in each case that year. I didn't bother with label approval. I got only one e-mail about it, but I heard that it squeezed some people kinda hard. It was nice to be able to say and share those words on my own label. There was something about it that seemed intimate, which is surely pretty counterintuitive when you're talking about a beer label, but that was what that space on that glued-on slip of paper was becoming.

> Have you ever said goodbye to an old dog? She could've been a mutt but she was one of a kind, and maybe you even found her at a garage sale. Maybe she belonged to your girlfriend and, the way some dogs will, she watched the first time you made love. Maybe she remembered that time for the both of you. Maybe she first belonged to someone who isn't here anymore either. Maybe she once loved a lost parent, or had been around so very long that she remembers when you were still young and understood little. Maybe you remembered the same for her. Maybe she always accepted what you also loved, even if they were cats. Maybe as she grew older and weaker she became an even more beautiful animal, and maybe you didn't always properly recognize this, and she never thought twice about it. Maybe she was just one piece in the puzzled mosaic of a busy life, but she was a key piece. Maybe she had a name like Chelsea, or Fuzzy, or Gypsy, or Blue, and we will always, always miss her.
> MARCH, 1981–SEPTEMBER, 1998.

On and on the flavor and label explorations went, each label and beer flavor building on the next. It was a good and creative time. We even began messing with our more legitimate beer descriptions. The larger beer fests, like the Oregon Brewers Fest, all do event programs complete with sponsor ads and participating breweries, with a brewery-prepared description of each beer being offered for tasting. One year we sent a description that read something like: "Lagunitas IPA boasts the aromas of stagnant pond water, delivering the rank flavors of broccoli, kerosene, and burning tractor tires." Why not? I have always admired the brilliant confidence of the rockin' band Primus's self-imposed "slogan": "Primus sucks." It took me quite a while to build up the nerve to brand anything with "Lagunitas Sucks," but I finally made the leap in 2011 with the Lagunitas Sucks Brown Shugga' Substitute Ale.

I've often been very humbled by the nature of the relationship that brewers have with their consumers. Beer, like maybe only cigarettes and communion wafers, is taken on faith by its consumers. The bottle is very often opened and the titillating liquid taken into the recipient's body sight unseen, ingested, and savored deeply, then it migrates through tissues and into the blood on its way directly to the brain to make it warm and even make it do tricks, to the delight of the communicant. This trust in our product feels like a very nearly sacred responsibility to me. There is more than just a flavor and a buzz in brewing; building a beer brand is like building an invisible existential pleasure palace. All of this has given us the confidence to blaze our own trail with our brand, while we took the people who were interested and willing along for the ride. It's been a trip of discovery for both sides, and I have always felt that this shared trip has created a tribe of real fans, with whom we have a real relationship.

This pretty much brings us to the 2009 Correction Ale (we weren't able to proclaim a 2010 Recovery Ale, but instead we did a Wilco Tango Foxtrot Ale—as in WTF?—about the oxymoronic jobless recovery). In 2009 we first brewed our future super-starlet, the Little Sumpin' Sumpin' Ale, and its big sister, the Little Sumpin' Extra! Ale, and their crazy cousin, the Little Sumpin' Wild Ale (made with a wild Belgian-type yeast strain). These were all experimental brews for us, playing with new hops and brewing techniques and such. Both the beers and the labels were dug by many, based on how they sold in the world and from the e-mails that came in over the brewery's transom. But for all of the good responses, the 2009 Correction and the Little Sumpin' Sumpin' Ales did elicit two critical e-mails.

On the 2009 I borrowed a favorite line from the movie *Animal House* that went, "And yes, we took some liberties with some of our female guests," using the "female guests" as a metaphor for the, well, whorishly debt-ridden and excessive ways some of us had grown accustomed to living (those of us in Washington, especially) that led to the whole 2008–2009 meltdown. "It happened, and it was what it was," was all I meant. But a good guy named Don took me literally, and so did a nice lady named Nancy, who also took exception to the female image on the Little Sumpin' Sumpin' label. The lady on the label is actually sorta Susan Sarandon–cute, but maybe the leggy hot pants were somehow offensive?

I do realize that if one person writes something, a lot more people probably are thinking it. Maybe I should have been more circumspect in the language, but I showed it to my wife and other women in the office, and they usually tell me if something smells bad about a label. They all liked it. Maybe it is good to get people riled up from time to time. Maybe.

We enjoyed the hijinks around the whole process of playing with our brand and having fun with our customers. But I think it's worth pointing out that while we were doing all that stuff, we maintained a laser-like focus on relentlessly presenting our Lagunitas IPA to the world. Our IPA in 2009 represented just more than one-half of all the IPA sold in California. IPA is the real business we are in, and it is just greater than half of our brewery's total production today. All our other fun products help to serve as a pilot light under our IPA and keep the air around us fresh and fun.

At the end of the day, it is all part of the ongoing development of our skills and insights as brewers and brand builders, as well as a way of showing more of ourselves to the world. We do all of this in the hope that if we are honest and authentic in our approach to living and working, it will show in the brand. The brand is the lens that beer lovers look through to understand us and maybe see a little of themselves as well. It is good to have friends.

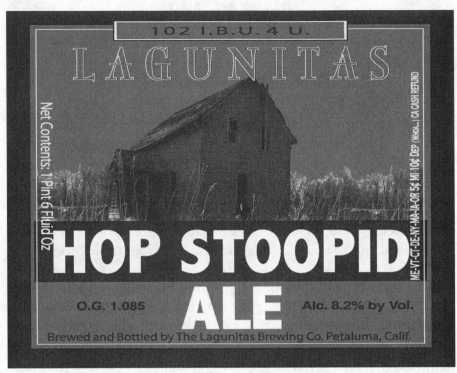

102 I.B.U. 4 U.

LAGUNITAS

Net Contents: 1 Pint 6 Fluid Oz

ME-VT-CT-DE-NY-MA-IA-OR 5¢ MI 10¢ DEP (WHOL.) CA CASH REFUND

HOP STOOPID ALE

O.G. 1.085   Alc. 8.2% by Vol.

Brewed and Bottled by The Lagunitas Brewing Co. Petaluma, Calif.

First Brewed in February, 2005

"Clean this mess up else we'll all end up in jail... those test tubes and the scale... just get 'em all outta here..." He was referring to the complex super-critical-CO2 hop extraction equipment set up on the table in the lab across from the brewhouse. Hop extracts are for the BIG brewers, he thought- suitable only for crummy sub-standard and barely-passable industrial lagers, not the subtle and elegant craft beer made here. But wrong he was. The New-Brewer does not eschew any possible inputs. In this case the extract will replace the mountains of hop vegetative material in the kettle thus creating cleaner hop flavors and preventing the otherwise spinach-like mess of a kettle full of super-hopped wort from clogging up a pump or worse. The sensuous honey-like amber ooze was administered intravenously to the wort kettle and the sacrament was complete. Another kettle of Hop Stoopid is once again raised up and fermented on high. Call us!

...The Banned Version...

"Give it to Mikey... He'll drink anything..!'" Up the bomber went in toast, then to his lips, and what happened next could not have been foreseen. Hop Stoopid, a slick re-animator greenish fluid oozed from the bottle. When it crossed his teeth and came in contact with the bitterness flavor receptors on his tongue, his eyes rolled back in his head, he did a sort of death rattle, a cloud crossed the Sun, and all his hair fell out. A spot on the side of his cheek blistered and a little bit of juice squirted out laterally starting a small fire. The rest of his head did the Indiana Jones melting Nazi thing, and as his head drained down his shirt and into the open stump of his esophagus a little whistling noise came from his navel, which burst open and squirted some goo onto his pals, one in the forehead and the other in the eye. Finally, the carcass slumped forward in a gelatinous mess, caught fire, and burned for three weeks. Let's talk. Call us!

DOWN WITH DOGMA

One time I was on an old-fashioned LISTSERV for a big Pacific Northwest home-brewing club. One of their members sent me a private e-mail asking what style one of our seasonals was intended to be. I had never thought about that particular beer in terms of style; it just was as it was, so I placed my tongue firmly in my cheek and replied, "It is a traditional Uzbeki Raga Ale." The next day, the LISTSERV forum received a post from the fellow I'd responded to complaining that my sarcasm was inappropriate and had no place in brewing, and that it was disrespectful of the ancient art and, and, and. Well, all hell broke loose. The thread went on for a week, back and forth, for and against. I held my fingers off the keyboard. Dogma and style and rigidly defined areas of doubt must form a backbone of security for many people, but they are chains to me.

I was recently asked to write a brewer's column for a really cool beer magazine. The magazine has a very active Internet reviewing site, and many of their most active online reviewers are very intense beer folk. I'm trying to be nice here. The publishers told me I could write anything I wanted, and so I reread some of the previous pieces in earlier editions written by other brewers. I had nothing. I can't play ball that way. I just don't write seriously about what we do. Finding myself stuck, I recalled a 150-page thing I'd assembled of the nonsense verbiage that you sometimes find at the bottom of spam e-mails, which spammers use to "dilute" the word count in order to sneak their spam through the spam filters. Sometimes they are fragments of quotes, sometimes random words—all meaningless. Some of it is brilliant, if only accidentally. I think of it as dadaist poetry, or as a form of "anti-communication." So—and I got this idea from my dad—I went through it all and pulled out some juicy bits and assembled five hundred words' worth of basic nonsense. I put it through a spell-checker, then a grammar-checker, and accepted whatever corrections Bill Gates proposed. I then peppered it with some brewing jargon, and (drumroll, please) voila! I had a five-hundred-word essay that I could get behind. It was not a prank. In fact, by the time I was done with it, I noticed it seemed like it was trying to actually say something from the depths of my unconscious, albeit in code, sort of like a Ouija board.

The publisher was good to his word and published it as is. A four-day, 120-comment riot broke out the next morning on the magazine's website. Halfway through the postings, the publisher of the magazine posted a comment calling for calm and civility, to no avail. I worried that a lynch mob was on its way to the brewery, and I laid low for a couple of weeks. Again, I say: beer speaks; people (me) mumble. In any case, they say there's no such thing as bad press, right? I also once read on the back of a Slash Records punk compilation that for early punk bands "just being bad led to apathy—but being truly hated required something special." Word. Did we digress?

Beer labels and the point-of-sale material produced are all under the oversight of the Alcohol and Tobacco Tax and Trade Bureau (TTB), and the TTB does not have much of a sense of humor. Labels in particular must be submitted for their approval before they can be used. The approval process has guidelines, but the implementation can be pretty darn subjective. For instance, you cannot use the word *quaffed* because it suggests overindulgence. I once used the word *piss* on a sort of free-verse thing ("running down the piss anvil cop car donut head possibility and the promise of bread"), and it was denied on the grounds that we shouldn't use language that we wouldn't use in polite company. I don't think my mom drinks our beer, let alone reads the labels, but at least the reasoning was genteel.

Early on, they told me I needed to remove the "Contains no actual insects" from the Bug Town Stout label because it suggested that other beers *did* contain actual insects. They finally relented on that one. In the great and weird state of Texas you can't, on a beer label, call beer, uh . . . well . . . "beer" if it is above four-point-something in alcohol, because if it is, then the beer, uh, I mean, well, the "not beer," must be called "ale." They think that calling it "beer" will confuse consumers. I don't know what that says about Texans, but it confuses *me*.

Nowhere in the USA can you call a beer Kronik, but after it is rejected, you can call it Censored. Strangely, someone managed to call a kid's energy drink Kronik after we were denied the name. The energy-drink industry clearly isn't as regulated. When the TTB rejected *our* use of the evil word *Kronik*, I called and had a long conversation with the regulator. They're not trolls; they are cops, and they have a number of different databases they consult for feedback on various suspect terms. It was the NIH's database of street language that narc'd out Kronik. But the thing that made the word suspect enough to investigate was a summer intern working in their office who noticed the paperwork on a desk awaiting processing. Had he not noticed it, it likely would have been approved. While talking with the regulator, I pointed out the obvious and equally reproachable use of the word *Bud* on a label and asked him what his database said about that. I pointed out the clear inference in High Life and that Redhook was a new and really strong variety of pot grown in the Pacific Northwest. (I just plain made that one up, but he was interested to learn more about it just the same.)

On the bottom of the Kronik six-pack was a long ramble that read in a decidedly Jeff Spicoli–esque tone. At first I was supposed to remove that too, because it suggested an "intoxicated state" (duh), but after the name Kronik was changed to Censored, the Spicoli-speak was all cool. Whatever.

It's all become a big cat-and-mouse game between reality and the TTB. Related things do sometimes get approved, like the suggestive 420 Extra Pale Ale, Hemp Ale, Weed ales, Indica India Pale Ale, Train Wreck Amber Ale, Eight-Ball Stout, the ugly word *Bastard*, and all sorts of others . . . even our own Brown Shugga'. When I named that beer, I was actually thinking of the song of the same name, and there really is a lot of brown sugar in the brew, but the name also alludes to an older double entendre for a problematic drug. Seems there wasn't anyone in the TTB office old enough to recognize that one.

Most strangely, I learned that the word *romance* is verboten because it suggests a health effect. What? This subversive word was on our Olde GnarlyWine label for many years in an adaptation of the Japanese tea ceremony verse: "The first sip is for thirst, the second for pleasure, the third for romance, and the fourth for madness." Then one year we resubmitted it, and it was rejected. I asked the nice lady on the phone who signed the rejection if she had ever been in a romance. They are not healthy, and you might do a lot of crazier things under the influence of romance than you might do under the influence of alcohol! No matter, the answer was no. So I changed it to "the third [sip] is for knowing" and that was OK with them. The irony? When I came up with the alternative word *knowing*, I was thinking about the second-date-if-you're-lucky-payoff-to-the-romance carnal kind of "knowing." Goes to show you never can tell.

On our GnarlyWine label I also wrote:

> Making a mondo ultra mega super premium barleywine is a lot like having a kid. The first part is fun and messy, it takes a while to ferment, and a while longer to mature, and you worry whether or not you'll still be friends when it grows up. Eventually it stays out all night and wrecks the car . . .

No go. Talking about wrecking the car could be promoting drunk driving. Incredulous, I changed the sentence to, "Eventually it stays out all night and comes home with its skirt on backwards . . ." That went over fine. Go figure. Drunk driving is out; teen sex is in. I suppose I can live with that.

Equally strange was the TTB's complete rejection of the original story on the side of the Hop Stoopid twenty-two-ounce bottle that read as follows:

"Give it to Mikey. . . . He'll drink anything. . . ." Up the bomber went in toast, then to his lips, and what happened next could not have been foreseen. Hop Stoopid, a slick re-animator green fluid, oozed from the bottle. When it crossed his teeth and came in contact with the bitterness flavor receptors on his tongue, his eyes rolled back in his head, he did a sort of death rattle, a cloud crossed the sun, and all his hair fell out. A spot on the side of his cheek blistered and a little bit of juice squirted out laterally starting a small fire. The rest of his head did the Indiana Jones melting Nazi thing, and as his head drained down his shirt and into the open stump of his esophagus, a little whistling noise came from his navel, which burst open and squirted some goo onto his pals, one in the forehead and the other in the eye. Finally, Mikey's carcass slumped forward in a gelatinous mess, caught fire, and burned for three weeks.

The TTB's explanation was that indicating what will happen to a person if they drink the beer—even saying that you will dissolve and catch fire—is a "health claim," and therefore verboten. Well then, here's to your health!

There were lots and lots of strange encounters with the TTB over our labels because I guess we really are feeling for the edges a lot of the time. Eventually the TTB guys and gals told me that they always enjoy our labels, but they do look at them a little closer than they do most others because of the obvious feeling-around-for-the-edges thing. I guess if they aren't talking about you, you aren't trying hard enough.

But still, we digress.

With so many breweries making so many new beers, it's inevitable that there will be unintentional overlap and duplication. It is inconceivable, given the brash creativity that seems innate to just about every new craft brewer, that there would be genuine name-stealing. Once, we quickly named a beer XS Ale (as in, "too much of a good thing") and it was quickly written up in a Portland, Oregon, newspaper. That seemed good. I Googled "XS" over the weekend to see if our beer had been listed on one of the beer-rating sites (I had to look; I never want to know, but I gotta look), and up came about three pages of search results for Rogue Ales. I felt terrible. I should have at least done a quick web search on the name before it went out, but I was running too fast for my own good and blew off that crucial step. Knowing the Portland paper was going to write about it that next Monday, I called up Rogue's owner and caught him walking his dog. He wasn't happy, but he was basically cool. We talked, I apologized, said I'd change things right away, sent him an official letter telling him that was the case, and we have never been anything but friendly since. That is what I like about craft brewing.

However, another brewer genuinely accused me of plagiarism one time, and it was as surprising as it was offensive. Maybe right now you're saying to yourself that I'm careless and stupid. Well, I can be both. But in business you make so very many decisions, tiny and large, that they get to be hard to differentiate sometimes. Especially when you're careless and stupid like I am. In this particular case, we had made a beer named after our favorite constitutional amendment, which says: "The enumeration of rights [here] shall not be construed to deny or disparage others retained by the people." In other words: "If a power is not given here (in the constitution) to a branch of government, then it (the power) is retained by the people (you and me)." There it is: Power to the people! First declared in faraway 1791. It seems to be the most forgotten, overlooked, and trod-upon part of our constitution. But it is also part of a cool piece of music, your partners part of sixty, a yin's yang, and other minor and significant numerological references.

It also happens to be another brewer's registered trademark on the far side of the country from Lagunitas. Mea culpa. I didn't know. I should have done a simple Google check then too, but I didn't. We made the beer as a seasonal and sold it. A little later, I received a call from a guy who said he owned a brewery and a federal trademark on that name, and he wanted me to stop using it. I finally did Google it while we were talking, and realized that I'd been careless and stupid. I told him that it would be easy to fix the situation, especially since it was a seasonal and the inventory had sold out already, and that next year we'd certainly rename it.

All seemed well after that conversation. The material thing about protecting trademarks is to prevent consumers being confused and the owner of a trademark from losing the value of his/her own work. Neither of us sold beer in each other's markets, and the overlap went on for a whole of about two months. The real likelihood of consumer confusion was pretty small. But about two months later I received a very threatening letter from the same brewer's attorney, declaring that I had lied, that we were still making the label, and that they'd gotten evidence of such directly from my own marketing manager. The letter further stated that they had uncovered evidence that undeniably linked my wife and me to drug abuse and payoffs as part of a San Joaquin Valley smut ring!

I stared dumbfounded while the tone of the letter sunk in. I asked my marketing manager what they could possibly be referring to. He thought about it, and recalled getting an e-mail from a consumer a couple of weeks earlier raving about that now-gone seasonal and asking where he could get more. My manager had referred the writer to a local warehouse retailer who stocks larger inventories and might still have some lying around. Again I stared dumbfounded as it sank in that the e-mail had been sent to check up on my honesty, and that they'd assumed an awful lot from an awful little.

I was pretty insulted. I called up the attorney who sent the letter, and she condescendingly explained how they had indeed snared me in my lie and said that they were going to take unspecified action to protect their property that I had tried to make off with. Have you ever felt rage boil up from somewhere genuinely primal? I have, and I did. I told her, in so many kind words, to knock it the hell off and not to bother me again. I also e-mailed the brewer directly and told him plainly that he should be ashamed of himself. He called me on the phone and began the conversation with: "Let me tell you how this works," and told me that I should try to be a little more creative rather than just trying to see what I could get away with. The tirade continued, including a claim that I had even tried to copy his super-sexy recipe for their clearly special beer, about which I must have been understandably jealous.

For the record, the recipe he was defending was/is a fruit-flavored beer. The only thing that I have ever done at the brewery for which I am truly ashamed—and the shame is profound—is having made that one seven-barrel batch of Peach Wheat (it was actually apricot). We have always since had a mantra at Lagunitas:

Eat the fruit, smoke the herb, drink the beer. Don't mix.

I stood wrongly accused of being so bereft of an imagination that I had to steal a beer name *and* a recipe, and worse—it was a (gasp) fruit beer. Aaack! That was a genuine existential crisis. I thought to myself, *How can I go on?* I took deep breaths. I visualized world peace. I was sure I would require therapy. You know how some conversations just make you feel like you need to take a shower?

Coincidentally, this same brewer would later figure into our deal with the Zappa estate, wherein we would brew a beer for each record created by the legendary Frank Zappa, but on the *genuinely* unauthorized borrowing end of the stick. You can easily discern what someone is most guilty of by observing what they accuse others of. More on this later, but the wheel does seem to go round.

For the record, I know that there are at least a few other brewers around the country, pubs mostly, with beer names that are either identical or very similar to some of ours, and it doesn't bother me as much as my attorney says it should. It's better to have friends. And if it got to be a problem, I think we could come up with a more interesting name that would wear the story of the process of its becoming on its sleeve—just like this one!

Over the intervening years we slung a whole bunch of experimental recipes and labels into the market—some successful, some less so. Someone once said that in business you only need to be right three times out of ten to succeed. That sounds like a low average until you consider that a career of batting .333 earns you a plaque in Cooperstown. In my experience, it rings true. We made all kinds of never-again-to-be-seen beers: the Old Ale, Ragwater, Peach Wheat, the Not-Quite-A-PILS, the Eye of the Hairball, the Lagunator, Joseph's

Best Brown Ale, the Satinugal and Mehapovet Ales, the Rye Porter, the Radicchio-Bok-Choy Ale, the Osama bin Lager, the Cubist Triple Ale, Sirius Ale . . . the list goes on a little bit further. But all that experimenting had an upside, and we learned more than a little bit about brewing and about feeling around for the edges. When things go well, you learn almost nothing. In failure there is learning.

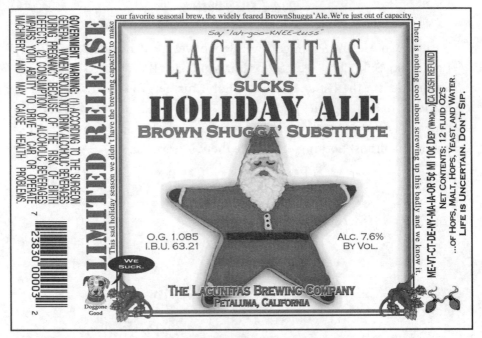

LIMITED (LITER) RELEASE

This sad holiday season we didn't have the brewing capacity to make

our favorite seasonal brew, the widely feared BrownShugga'Ale. We're just out of capacity.

There is nothing cool about screwing up this badly and we know it.

Say "lah-goo-KNEE-tuss"

LAGUNITAS
SUCKS
HOLIDAY ALE
BROWN SHUGGA' SUBSTITUTE

O.G. 1.085
I.B.U. 63.21

ALC. 7.6%
BY VOL.

WE SUCK.

THE LAGUNITAS BREWING COMPANY
PETALUMA, CALIFORNIA

Doggone Good

ME-VT-CT-DE-NY-MA-IA-OR 5¢ MI 10¢ DEP (WHOL... CA CASH REFUND
NET CONTENTS: 12 FLUID OZ'S
...OF HOPS, MALT, HOPS, YEAST, AND WATER.
LIFE IS UNCERTAIN. DON'T SIP.

7 23830 00003 2

First Brewed in September, 2011

*T*his sad holiday season we didn't have the brewing capacity to make our own very most favorite seasonal brew, the widely feared BrownShugga'Ale. You see, we had a couple of really good years (thank you very much) and so heading into this season while we are awaiting the January delivery of a new brewhouse we are jammin' along brewing 80 barrels of IPA and PILS and such every 3 hours. A couple months back we realized that since we can only brew a mere 60 barrels of Shugga' every 5 hours, that we were seriously screwed. For every case of Shugga' brewed, we'd short 3 cases of our favorite daily beers. It's a drag. This year, we brewed something that we think is also cool and brews more like our daily brews. The new brewhouse will help insure that this kind of failure never occurs again. It's a mess that we can not brew our BrownShugga' this year and we suck for not doing it. There is nothing cool about screwing up this badly and we know it. Maybe we can sue our own sorry selves. There is no joy in our hearts this holiday and the best we can hope for is a quick and merciful end. F%@k us. This totally blows. Whatever. We freaking munch moldy donkey butt and we just want it all to be over...

THE EXPERIMENTAL RECIPES

YOU WIN SOME, YOU LOSE SOME

*B*ack on the brand front, I came to realize in 2005 that we had lost some freedom with respect to recipes. Lagunitas has gained a certain good reputation among consumers for making beers that have bigger flavors, which is great, but it makes it a little difficult to market more delicately flavored beers. They are dismissed as feeble and go nowhere. Being delicate without being daring is not bad, but it has become a little uncool. It is like Elvis Costello singing Burt Bacharach songs; it is too much of a disconnect from fans' expectations. But I still wanted the freedom to experiment with the light side. So in 2007 we worked up a recipe for a very nice somewhat French-styled ale made with our house Belgian yeast strain.

I could imagine what would happen if we marketed it as a mainline Lagunitas release. So to make a little space for the beer to speak for itself, I did up a whole other branded label for it and called it Sonoma Farmhouse Saison Style Ale by Lagunitas. The beer was loved by non-beer-crazy types who simply wanted an interesting flavor without all the horsepower, but the big beer geeks eschewed it. "One for the sink to drink," one review said. Beer reviewers can be worse than high school girls sometimes. But they are also demanding and want to be impressed.

Unfortunately, the Saison didn't sell well initially because I mistakenly put it in twenty-two-ounce bottles, and the sort of people who liked it don't really shop the bomber section too much. I was worried about it holding the shelf space long enough to be discovered by folks who might like it, so I worked up another brew that would help hold the Saison's spot on the shelf, and we called it Hop Stoopid, also under the Farmhouse label. The labels were very European-ish (I based the look on a traditional brie-wheel label) and, I thought, cool-looking, so I was proud of the whole look and feel. The Hop Stoopid just took off (it was big, very hoppy), and it won raves while its more delicate cousin got run over, pissed on, and stomped back into the terra firma from which it came. So, sadly, we let the Saison label die a quiet death, and the Hop Stoopid label was modified a little to bring it into the Lagunitas family label look. So much for extracurricular excursions. We'll just stick to our knitting and do what we are known for. But even in this instance of seeming failure, I batted .500, well ahead of the .333 the wonks say is good enough!

Once, an online interviewer asked me how we come up with new beers to release. I told him that coming up with interesting recipes is actually the easy part. We are always dreaming of things we'd like to experiment with. For the record, we don't have a pilot plant. When we brew something new, we brew eighty barrels of it, minimum, but more likely we brew three hundred barrels of it. I like to think we got skills!

The hard part is discovering the name of the beer. We know how to brew good beer, but it is the name that animates the liquid and gives it a voice. The flavor comes afterward, to the consumer, and it must live up to their expectations, but first there is the name. If the beer really does speak, the label is the first sentence.

It is an interesting thing to have a blank label always available to think onto, and I am always looking for that seed of imagination that inspires a new beer. Sometimes it comes from unexpected sources. It is widely known that we had the California Department of Alcohol Beverage Control (ABC), the state alcohol regulatory agency, in the brewery trying to buy pot from my employees. In fact, when some unknown person did us the favor of writing a Wikipedia entry, that particular event was the sole nugget they chose to highlight about us. The ABC visited our Thursday Night Open House night and they saw smoke, so they were sure that if they didn't see a fire, they could build one for us. A sting was hatched. The effort to get an employee to sell them some pot didn't work, and they left empty-handed, except for an allegation against our license that I ran a "disorderly house." I'll discuss that in nauseating detail later on, but suffice to say that I/we did the crime, I/we did the time, I/we get the bragging rights. And where better to brag than on your own beer label?

I have always thought that you don't need to defuse a bomb that has already gone off, so rather than have the world speak in whispers about what they heard about our "difficulties," I'd just take the lead and make our feelings known, so that consumers and everyone else might hear it from the horse's mouth. It's *our* brand, we can speak for ourselves, and the label is like a tiny broadcast station to speak from. The particular beer that I'm alluding to—the Undercover Investigation Shut-Down Ale—was intentionally designed to reflect the experience: aggressive and bitter, a fermented punch in the mouth. The ale did well in the world, and in commemoration it is re-brewed every spring. As the label says, "We're still here."

Lots of breweries talk about how irreverent they are, but how many take a punch and get back up to piss on their antagonist's shoes . . . and do it in public? I think we rock. Of course, we will never, never, ever, do anything like that ever, ever again. Honest. Really. No, really. Honest.

One of the more successful adventures off of the reservation started in 2008 with the Zappa album cover labels. I have been a Frank Zappa fan ever since 1980 or so, when my future wife introduced me to his music in college. I was studying music composition, and he was probably the most energetic composer with a beating heart. His music was as unprecedented then as I hope Lagunitas is now. One afternoon in 2006 I wondered if the record company that had acquired the Zappa catalog in the 1990s (and has since lost control of said catalog to the Zappa Family Trust), Rykodisc, would be interested in licensing the album cover art so we could use it as a commemorative bottle label. The idea wasn't at all an effort to find a way to sell more beer. We were already at that year's production capacity, but I hoped it would be fun, and I knew it would be a great honor. I wanted to connect with others who also loved the music, and I hoped that maybe I would have a chance to meet the Zappa family.

I tried to call and write to Rykodisc for a couple of weeks with no response. So I took a wild guess as to what Gail Zappa's e-mail address might be, sorta like random dialing, and it worked. The next day, I got a reply, and things began. I didn't realize it at the time, but that year was coincidentally the fortieth anniversary of the release of *Freak Out!* (the landmark first Mothers of Invention album). It was unbelievable; we were in business with the Zappa Family Trust (ZFT). We made a verbal agreement about the production quantities and the fee Lagunitas would pay, and we were off. The very fact that we only ever had a verbal agreement with the Zappa people was a source of great pride for me. Being trusted by my heroes was a big deal. I've done many, many important deals for the brewery on a handshake. A couple of years ago I bought our new brew house from a Bavarian company on a handshake. There is nothing better, in my book. It was an amazing thing to see the album-cover art that Frank Zappa himself had worked on and approved flowing down my bottling line, embellishing my own work. I felt like I was in the presence of true greatness—or at least as close as I would ever come. Five hundred years from now, Zappa's music still will be listened to, long after Lagunitas is forgotten. This seemed to me like an intimate moment in his presence.

The Zappa beer was a hop stew that gave us a chance to experiment with some different ingredients like toasted wheat, new hop varieties, cocoa nibs, white pepper, and our house Belgian yeast strain. Freak Out! was very successful and did everything I'd hoped it would to connect Zappa lovers. I received e-mails from all over the world, and I saw empty bottles being sold on eBay.

A few weeks after the release of Freak Out!, I got a phone call from a cool guy in L.A. who worked at the original Alligator Records store in Claremont. He said that he was calling on behalf of a friend, Ray Collins, who was the original singer for the Mothers of Invention (in fact, it started out as his band) and that it would mean a lot to him if I could send some labels down. I was going to be in L.A. in a couple of

Jeremy Marshall, head brewer

I hope to create beer that is unique, but also simple. Beer need not be pretentious; it is still the working man's drink, and craft beer is the thinking working man's drink.

We really are who we appear to be: punk rockers, misfits, hippies, Ivy Leaguers, weirdos, geeks, Waldos, Zappa freaks, sparkle ponies, musicians, rednecks, Burners, festivators, jocks, animal lovers, and mullet enthusiasts. There's not a huge difference between the behind-the-scenes and the brand (that's called "authenticity," I've heard). Sure, we have our fair share of drama and misery, but most of that is universal to breweries, and ours is unique because dogs run around everywhere, and cats too, though the cats were here before us.

Lagunitas has become a success through careful decision making, being truthful to itself and its customers, being dependably unpredictable, and very importantly, by re-investing constantly in the plant and its people. No ATM machine here; it's all about the beer. Things have changed; certain things have to end if a company is going to grow up. I suppose 420 breaks every 15 minutes are fine in high school, but sooner or later too much is jeopardized by being whimsically cavalier all the time.

As for my favorite brew, it depends what season it is and what mood I'm in. Kill Ugly Radio was a good one, but I also have nostalgia for Imperial Red. Lagunitas Sucks was fun for us, as we'd not really brewed with much alternate grains before. Seems like craft [brewing] in general has a love affair with these unusual seeds, which is great, since hops get most of the glam, but please don't forget the barley farmers, eh?

weeks, so we made a plan to meet. Ray turned out to be a very sweet and soulful guy, and it was a great visit. Unfortunately, the early Mothers of Invention band members and the ZFT are not really on speaking terms over conflicts endemic to the music-industry business. Sometimes I think that the term "music industry" is an oxymoron. They really are mutually exclusive words. Nonetheless, it made strangers of the early band and the ZFT. Eventually even the brewery was sucked down into this historical muck a little.

Many months later, after the Cruising with Ruben & the Jets commemorative brew was released, Ray Collins called me again from a pay phone, pumping quarters into it while we spoke. I might point out that it is possible Ray—who sadly passed away on December 24, 2012—did not have a permanent address, if you understand. He told me of the recent death of Jimmy Carl Black, the original drummer for the band. At a park just outside of L.A., a memorial concert and silent auction benefit was being planned by friends. The event was intended as a fundraiser for Black's widow and kids, who were also on hard times. I said I would be more than happy to offer a few cases of Ruben for the auction. I spoke with the ZFT later that week and mentioned the donation, and the news was not received well. Old injuries do not always heal, and that was the end of the Zappa series for us.

This brings up an interesting side note about the strangest confluence of interactions. It came about at the very end of the ZFT relationship. The ZFT asked me to do one more label, for the *Joe's Garage* album. At first I didn't understand, because it was out of the album/label release order we'd been using from the start. But then I remembered something. I'd known for a while that the ZFT was aware of another brewer who was using the name Joe's Garage as a clear reference to the album of the same name, only they were doing it without ever having called the ZFT to discuss it. It was the same brewery that I'd had the messy overlap with earlier. Can you imagine? I would guess the brewer called the brewery's lawyer—the same one who wrote me after the espionage e-mail that convinced them I was still purloining their trademark—and the lawyer told him that they didn't have to ask permission, mostly for technical reasons, which is sort of true. I guess they thought that they could "get away with it," as they had once accused *me* of doing. I declined to do the label because I didn't want to be in the middle of the argument, but it was amusing and duplicitous, to say the least. The wheel does go round.

All in all, the Zappa series was a personally proud moment. To have built an enterprise that could reach way up across from my current industry to my old aspirational career, and to earn the opportunity to work with Mrs. Gail Zappa, if only for a while, was cool. Over the last few years I have read lots of very thoughtless Internet chat-room comments about the ZFT legal dealings and its handling of Mr. Zappa's enormous legacy, but none of those people ever met any of the family in person, let alone while sitting in Zappa's own home studio. If you want to dislike someone, don't get to know them. If the chat-room trolls had ever met any of the Zappa family, they would have seen that the Zappas are very cool and kind people, and that the pressure of managing a global legacy is daunting. It is not a microscope that I would want to live under. But on the bright side, when asked about it, I've said that all good things come to an end, and sometimes that's the way you know if they were good to begin with. This project was very good indeed, and it'll surely make my highlight reel.

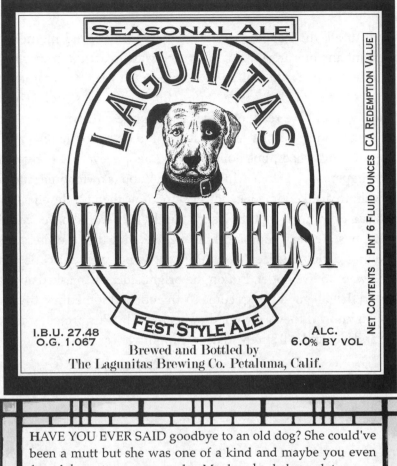

HAVE YOU EVER SAID goodbye to an old dog? She could've been a mutt but she was one of a kind and maybe you even found her at a garage sale. Maybe she belonged to your girlfriend and, the way some dogs will, she watched the first time you made love. Maybe she remembered that time for the both of you. Maybe she first belonged to someone who isn't here anymore either. Maybe she once loved a lost parent, or had been around so very long that she remembers when you were still young and understood little. Maybe you remembered the same for her. Maybe she always accepted what you also loved, even if they were cats. Maybe as she grew older and weaker she became an even more beautiful animal, and maybe you didn't always properly recognize this, and she never thought twice about it. Maybe she was just one piece in the puzzled mosaic of a busy life, but she was a key piece. Maybe she had a name like Chelsea or Fuzzy, Gypsy or Blue, and we will always, always, miss her.

March, 1981 - September, 1998

THE BREWERY

THE STORY OF THE PLACE ITSELF

*T*aking the story way back again to January 1993, the Lagunitas Brewing Company started out like most every craft brewery everywhere: on the tiny stove in the tiny kitchen in our tiny house in the tiny town of Lagunitas. It was never formally licensed there, but the first recipes and the company's conceptual existence began there. That stove finally caught fire from all the wort boilovers (two days before Thanksgiving, actually). Predictably, I was required to move the "brewery" to the porch, and later even further from the front door to 750 square feet of commercial space in the back of the old House of Richards Grocery Store building in West Marin's equally tiny Forest Knolls, some five thousand feet away.

It was actually the only available commercial space around that had a real concrete floor. I was so oblivious about what a brewery was going to require that I originally agreed to rent the front of that same building, until someone asked me in a random conversation how big a fermenter those wooden frame floors could support once full of liquid that weighs nine pounds per gallon. Fortunately, the back of the building was also available, and it had concrete floors. It is good to be lucky, even if only a little, and especially over and over again.

So I rented that initial space early in 1993 while all the license work was in process. During that period I brewed furiously on a ten-gallon three-tier brewery, using cut-up scrap-yard kegs for the hot liquor tank, a kettle, and a mash/lauter tun. There, I worked up the first very rough recipes, which included a pale ale, a wheat ale that was never brewed under the license, a red ale, and our Cappuccino Stout that we still brew today.

As I mentioned earlier the brew house unit was built by John Cross's company, CDC, from Porterville, in the southern Sierra Nevada mountains. John typically built standard three-vessel brew houses with Grundy Tanks modified into fermenters, but this unit was very different. It was built to be permanently installed in a shipping container bound for rural Russia, but then something went wrong involving the Russian Mafia. The brewery's permit was denied, the brewery's building burned down, and the prospective brewer was found in an alley wearing a sledgehammer. Needless to say, the brew house unit was never finished. It looked like a fifteen-foot-long stainless-steel washing machine and was all electric. It was a single unit with three vessels integrated into the one box, with all the plumbing and wiring internal as well.

In reality, it worked pretty well for a $5,000 brew house. Insane. These days we might have to spend that much for one flow meter. When we first installed it, I didn't appreciate the importance of installing a serious Earth Ground Stake, which would have been a good idea since the unit was kind of sketchy to start with. It was made of all conductive steel, and you were usually standing in a puddle whenever you touched it. It drew almost 150 amps full-time between the hot liquor, the pumps, and the twenty heating elements under the kettle. During shipping and installation, one of those electric heating elements shifted and made a dead short to the stainless-steel frame. That was revealed when we turned it on for the first time and the big magnetic contactor in the control panel went off like a shotgun, slamming on and off several times in succession and eventually tripping the breaker for the whole building. When it all stopped, people came running around from the front of the building and asked what was happening, because the streetlights were flashing on and off too. I eventually sold it (for $5,000!) to a winery in the Sierra Nevada foothills that wanted to make beer on the side. I have never had the nerve to go and visit it.

I eventually got the whole pico-brewery up and running by December 1993. I started with the two seven-barrel dish-bottomed Grundy Tanks as fermenters, but after a couple of months I needed more. The first of those was another Grundy Tank that I took to a welding shop near the brewery, and for some beer and a little cash, they cut the bottom dish off of it and welded on a nice cone. This allowed me to begin harvesting liquid-culture yeast rather than the bricks of dried yeast I had been using. The dry yeast was usable, but it was not very clean, and because of that, you could not use it to re-pitch subsequent batches. The new cone-bottom tank brought a big improvement in beer quality.

The next tank I got was a fourteen-barrel tank. In 1994 I went back to the same welding shop and asked the lead welder about building a cheap, stripped-down version of their standard pretty brew-couture brewpub fermenters. He said sure, he could build it during the weekend using surplus steel from the shop. Huh? He gave me a price: about one-third what I expected. I should have been more worried, but I needed the tank, and he was the lead guy, so I figured it must be cool. Probably? He said cash would be best, and I obliged.

They built the tank that weekend and told me to come Monday at 4:30 AM to pick it up. OK. I arrived at the building in the dark. The roll up door lifted, and in the dark of the interior, the tank appeared, hanging all crazy on the end of a forklift sling. They dropped it onto the flatbed trailer and I drove back to the brewery. The tank was a hideous meth-inspired, burnt-weld-splatter-encrusted, three-crooked-legged thing from the outside, but on the all-important inside, it was like baby's skin.

About three years later, I received a phone call from the owner of the shop, who started by telling me that he "knew what I did." I really didn't know, but ignorance was bliss. I asked him if he wanted some additional retroactive payment for it, and he said no. I asked, "Are you sure?" He said, "No." I said, "OK." (Which was good, because I didn't have any money anyway.)

Turns out that the guys who sold me the tank had "requisitioned" all the steel and used the shop after hours without permission. The welder later went to jail over something else, but when he got out they rehired him, and over beers one night he told the owner the story. Why, I'll never know, but we still have the tank today and we use it as a yeast propagator. It is probably my favorite. I will never sell that fugly little girl.

Digress we did . . .

As things went along and I added more accounts, I got to where I needed a helper. Actually, I needed a brewer so that I could maintain my income from my printing business on the side. One afternoon, a 6'4", 245-pound fellow presented himself at the door to the brewery (actually blocking the door, so I couldn't avoid talking to him even if I'd wanted to) and proclaimed that he was probably the most qualified brewer in all of West Marin. Who was I to argue? Anyway, he was a little scary. He was a strange guy in many awkward ways, but he was honest and willing to work hard, and he enjoyed the rough equipment. It was like a giant home-brew system to him, and I suppose that's really what it actually was. In the end, he left and went on to work for the National Park Service tracking radio-tagged bobcats and mountain lions on the Point Reyes National Seashore. From time to time, I'd see him standing on the West Marin back roads, oblivious to the traffic and the rest of the world, wearing his tracker headset and his Park Service khaki coat, gripping a handheld antenna set pointed at an unseen predator somewhere up in the endlessly rolling hills. He looked like a cross between Frankenstein and John Muir. He was a good brewer.

At that early stage, I had an idea that the brewery would be as much of a Bronze Age enterprise as possible, but without all the famine and disease. I wanted it to be rough-hewn and easy to build. The flavorless German Altbier yeast strain I was using typically settled extremely well, leaving a nice, slightly hazy but mostly bright beer after about fifteen days in the fermenter—which was good, since I didn't want to have to filter the beer.

One thing the brewery quickly taught me about the Bronze Age was that things were more unpredictable then. One week, late in June 1994, just before the Fourth of July weekend, something strange happened with our yeast. It refused to settle out after fermentation as it always had before, and the beer was way too cloudy to put into kegs.

We were making unfiltered beer, but this was far too messy. In hindsight, it could have been any number of inexperience factors at work, but each yeast strain has different behavioral characteristics, and while some that don't settle make a nice swirling sort of haze, ours clumped into quarter-inch little blobs that looked like the Jolly Green Giant had the runs. At best, it was sorta chunky.

I had not been filtering the beer up until that point, but suddenly I needed to figure out how to, because our distributor was out of beer and it was the Fourth of July! I called up to a company in Petaluma that sells most of the filters to the area wineries, and they did just happen to have a perfect small filter on hand, which was very unusual and fortunate, but I didn't have the $6,500 to take it off their hands. I described my production problem to their filtration specialist, and in one of those surprising moments of betting on good faith, I asked outright if they'd let me take it away then with a small deposit and pay the rest in sixty days. They said yes. I don't know for sure, but in all of my later dealings with them, I'd be surprised if they had ever done that before (or after) for anyone. They are just kind people and decided to pay into the good-karma pool. I'll never know, but as I've written elsewhere here, that sort of generous good fortune has followed the brewery into some unusual situations. I was very humble and thanked them profusely.

It was already 4:00 PM on a Wednesday when I called, so I hung up the phone and raced up to their shop in Petaluma to load the filter into my little pickup. With a pretty substantial forklift, they dropped it into the back. The dock guy asked me how I planned to get it off when I got it back to the brewery. It was about three feet tall and wide by six feet long, and probably weighed five hundred pounds. I was so preoccupied with solving the problem at hand that I hadn't thought it through to that point yet, but I told him I'd have some help on the other end.

When I got back to the brewery, it was after 6:00 PM, and there was nobody in sight. After scratching my head for a bit, I rigged up some two-by-eights to make a sort of skid to slide the equipment down. I just barely got the weight of it onto the boards and—*crack!*—I was falling off of the back of the truck bed along with the 500-pound filter, which was about to land sideways on my leg. The patron saint of brewers must have intervened, because somehow I slid out from under it just before it landed. I vaguely noticed that it was not on top of me, and I got up. It took everything I had just to stand the filter upright and maneuver it into the building. I could see that it was a little tweaked from the fall, and since I'd messed it up, I definitely had to find the money and pay for it, no matter what.

Truth is, I did not know where I'd get the money from. Then, and for years and years after, we were like deep-sea divers, and money was like oxygen. But I squeezed my printing jobs a little bit harder and did pay the supplier on time, and remained a good customer for many years after.

So bright and early Thursday morning we rigged up the filter and sterilized it and ran the first crystal-clear Lagunitas beer into kegs. The beer was very pretty, but a little innocence was lost. The Bronze Age was in the rearview mirror, and I delivered a 4:00 AM load to our distributor in time for the holiday deliveries.

Part of the county approval of my brewery use permit required the building owner to install a large engineered septic system. The old one dated back to the 1940s and was inadequate for any sort of use, never mind a brewery. Since the old system would be removed after the new one was installed, the county allowed me to use it in the meantime. I guess they figured it wouldn't matter if it failed. I'm not sure they were right. On more than a few occasions, during the kettle runoff, when you use more cooling water than you need or can store, my brewer ran that water to the drain and into the septic. The septic tank was used in common with several adjacent apartments, including one along the road that just happened to be below the holding tank's surface. The runoff water quickly flooded the tiny septic tank. So, in short order, the entire tank backed up into that little apartment. I wasn't there at the time, which gave me "plausible deniability" (a useful term over the years), but I can only guess what the scene was like. After this fecal unimagineableness occurred a few more times, we started to divert the runoff water straight to the grassy yard. Even though this was clear warm water, it wasn't a legitimate solution, but the new septic system was in the works, so we limped along.

The septic contractor had to dig a trench to divert the rainwater from up the hill so that it wouldn't flow through the leach field. That trench got to about ten feet deep as the pipe fell underground through the parking lot. The contractor then hit an enormous underground granite rock in the middle of the driveway. I mean, enormous. The rock was like the subterranean peak of Half Dome. The installation contract had a "rock clause" that then increased their hourly work rate threefold, and the work took about six weeks longer than planned. That was three weeks of a jackhammer bit powering through rock a mere fifteen feet from the brewery. It was unbelievable.

The owner of the building was in Asia on vacation. When he got back, there was a $90,000 "rock clause bill" waiting for him. To make matters worse, when the system was finally completed in August, the septic engineering company came out to make the final adjustments and sampled what we were putting into the drain. With a dull detachment, the engineer on-site told me, "This is bad." They pulled the plug on the whole thing. They told the owner and the county that they would not warranty the septic if I used it for the brewery—which is what it was engineered for and installed on behalf of.

The engineers had asked me months earlier what was going into the drain, and I told them it was 90 percent clear rinse water, which was true. It is still true today! But what I didn't know, and they didn't ask, was how strong that last 10 percent was. It's what is left in the bottom of the home-brew kettle after the boil: spent yeast, some waste beer from hoses, the stuff stuck to the top of the fermenter and such. It's so strong that even 10 percent would overwhelm the new $130,000 septic system. The building owner, the county, and the septic engineers all agreed—I had to go. I'd only been there for eight months. The county gave me ninety days, which was how long it would take for them to claw back my use permit.

First Brewed in March, 2006

From the first day of the first mash of the first recipe in the first brewhouse in the first space to this oasis 13 years on the road; we have worked hard to walk in the footsteps of our hero brewers- The Noble Brewer of the planet's only legal Steam Beer, and Oregon's Rebel Brewer from Newport. Thirteen years down the road, we have found our own voice as brewers but our admiration for those *Great Ones* has not dimmed even one bit. If we walked well down the hero's path ourselves, perhaps we too have been an inspiration for others, you never know. Beer still represents the the best in a Bronze Age business and we feel honored to have left our footprints on it's path as the present becomes a future history... while at the same time leaving our flavors on your buds. Thank you for your trust over the years and we hope you enjoy this specially brewed Hi-Gravity Auburn offering.

Speer Beaks, Meople Pumble!

13

MOVING TO PETALUMA

FRIENDS AND FRENEMIES AND PETTY TYRANTS

My *unrealistic dream of a truly rural Bronze* Age brewery was dissolving before my eyes. I had to think about either pulling the plug on the whole thing and cutting my losses and going back to being a printing *puta* with my tail between my legs, or saying "damn the torpedoes" and relocating. I didn't like the prospect of being embarrassed by the failure, so it was settled. In any case, I was sort of an innocent bystander in the whole thing, and I have always believed in principles over good sense, and being wiped from the scene by the carelessness of others seemed wrong, but the only revenge available was that of living well and succeeding in ways that would be visible. You need to find motivation wherever you can.

I picked Petaluma because it had a sewer system (as you might assume any major metropolis in 1994 would have, although that turned out to be an overstatement of the facts, as you'll find out later), it was in the next (and more permit-friendly) county, and because I liked the drive from my home in Lagunitas. Since that decisive moment, I have now driven that West Marin–to–Petaluma back road more than seven thousand times in six different cars, and I am still not tired of it. It is some of the loveliest land anywhere I have ever been. Check it out on Google Maps. It is so perfectly rural that the roads are named for their functions, including the one I took and still take every day: Point Reyes–Petaluma Road. On a bad commute day I might get stuck behind a hay truck or a manure truck. While driving those twenty-four miles to work, I've seen mountain lions, kestrels, bobcats, deer, possums, ospreys, coyotes, foxes, golden eagles, falcons, hawks, and discarded IPA bottles.

The actual disassembly of the little brewery and the move to Petaluma had to be done by my brewer, his new assistant, and my very cool father-in-law, because about that exact time, my other soon-to-be-former career required me to be in L.A. for business. Which was good, because I was earning the moolah needed to finish the move. I missed most of the actual move. But move we did, and ninety days later we were brewing in Petaluma.

When I first got wind that we might have to move, I contacted John Cross again to discuss something I knew I could not afford: a larger and somewhat better brew house. The Russian deal was a seven-barrel batch volume, and that was a lot of work for not much wort. Plus, it was electric and underpowered. I was thinking *big* this time (he said, facetiously.) Fourteen barrels! As I wrote earlier, for what reason I'll never exactly know, Saint John Cross offered to build it for me; all I would have to do was cover the interest on the materials and labor to build it. This made all sorts of other things possible. I've said it already: I eventually paid him the money I owed him, but I will never pay off the debt.

Meanwhile, my West Marin brewer moved on to other things, and his assistant, a very inventive mechanical guy from San Anselmo, stepped up to be head brewer. Actually, he was the only brewer. At that point we had two seven-barrel dish-bottom Grundy Tanks and one seven-barrel and one fourteen-barrel cylindroconical (cone on the bottom) tanks. We would filter right out of a fermenter and directly into a keg. Over the course of the next five years we would add a few more fourteen-barrel tanks, and then later cut the tops off nearly all of them and weld in extra sidewalls to increase their volume, buy horizontal dairy tanks to use as secondary fermenters, convert other dairy equipment for brewing, and engineer all sorts of other crazy MacGyver-style stuff.

We used the dairy tanks I found as secondary fermenters, which allowed for a lot of inexpensive growth. The dairy industry all around us was changing, and its economics necessitated dairymen to upgrade to two- and three-thousand-gallon milk tanks. That made dozens of those clean and cheap one-thousand-gallon tanks available almost overnight. I bought them up as they became available, and eventually we had about eight of them. The good guy who aligned me with all of those tanks eventually came aboard as Lagunitas's process engineer. It's good to have friends.

By the fall of 1994 I realized we would have to start bottling if we were going to economically grow into our new Petaluma space. Twenty-two-ounce bottles were the perfect fit for hand-filling. I saw an article in *Zymurgy* magazine (the home brewers' monthly bible) about how another good brewery in Fort Bragg had adapted a simple home-brewer-designed copper-and-brass fitting set into a four-head bottle filler. My friend Barbara Groom of Lost Coast had done something similar. It was time for a road trip to see what we could learn from their experiences. Barbara was very generous. We made diagrams and came home to build a new and improved model.

This has nothing to do with the story, but we drove up to look at Barbara's filler on the spectacular Highway 101 to Eureka through the famous Emerald Triangle in a way cool 1964 Buick Wildcat two-door hardtop that my wife had snagged for me as a birthday present, rescuing it from the crusher at the county recycling center where she worked. On the way back, a rod went through a sidewall of a cylinder. It was a standard (for 1964) big V8 engine, and one cylinder didn't stop the show, so we drove home blowing clouds of white smoke and putting water in the radiator from time to time. That car was so sweet, but the repair would have cost a couple thousand dollars, and I did not have it. It was just sad. But recently I bought an Acura NSX, so what the fuck, things turned out OK.

Back to the filler project. Using all kinds of stuff we bought at the hardware store, we built a genuine (and manual) home-brewer-inspired rinser-filler-crowner bottling line. It took five people eight hours to fill 240 cases. That works out to seven bottles per minute, which isn't very much. But it got us up and going, and it made a very stable bottled product. We still have that little homemade thing on display in our tasting loft as "Our Founder." It was better in many ways than our later Crown Cork & Seal bottle filler/capper machine.

Altogether it cost about $2,500 to build. We produced something very close to $1 million in finished product on that little marvel (there is a picture of it here somewhere). Every bottle was individually hand-rinsed, filled six-at-a-time, capped, and labeled by a cool Guatemalan woman who stayed with us until her years on Earth and the damp arthritic space of the cold brewery got in the way of her bones. These were by far the most innocent days for the brewery, when everything we did sold better than the last thing.

Later in 1995, we bought a used bright green 1964 World Tandem labeler from the now-gone Portland Brewing Co. They were growing too, and grew out of it, after getting it originally from Sierra Nevada, which had also grown out of it. This labeler was a crazy bit of '60s technology, with one motor generating thirty or so different motions just to get the label on the bottle. Given its provenance, I though it was good juju having it in the brewery. To fill the twelve-ounce bottles, we also bought a compact four-head twelve-ounce filler/capper from David Meheen, a little upstart company out of Pasco, Washington. David hooked me up with a guy out of Redlands, California, with money and an interest in small breweries. He was doing private leases to breweries, and for some reason he decided we were OK and bought a machine for me. Later, he bought us another too, and he got his money back, with lots of interest, I think.

When I bought the second Meheen filler to run in parallel I thought we'd be twice as productive, but with entry-level machines like that, one plus one is not always two. It was a crazy natal period for the brewing plant. It seemed big, but I knew it was tiny and running so very hard to get anything done. We grew from six hundred barrels in 1994 to ten thousand barrels by 1998. We needed stuff, and lots of it. The brewery made lots of friends during that period, and we found lots of experts in different fields eager to help out, in part just because it was such an exciting place to hang out. The people working there were all very colorful, and the energy level was always at the limit.

We had a great pump guy get us set up with the twenty or so food-grade pumps we had no idea we'd need (those little things are thousands of dollars each). We had a friend who was a machinist, another a welder, another an electrician, another a plumber . . . on and on. Lots of times we were able to trade a couple of cases of beer for things like engineering drawings and architectural drawings, refrigeration repairs and floor epoxy, roofing work and electrical motor rewinding, bands and sound systems, and, and, and. I'm sure many small breweries around the country know this story. I've often thought that having a little brewery is a lot like being the only guy in a prison with cigarettes!

Eventually we filled nearly the entire eighty-five hundred square feet of the building in Petaluma, but it was all broken up into little spaces and was like working in a rabbit warren. We finally obtained a little bank financing and bought a whirlpool and a hot-water system for the brew house. Quickly, we were knocking out six brews each day. We cut the tops off more tanks and added even more sidewalls to them and increased our capacity in a hundred small ways, substituting creativity for cash at every turn. It was a good policy.

Early on in the brewery days, I'd read Paul Hawken's book *Growing a Business*. In it, he opines that while conventional wisdom says that most small businesses fail for a lack of capital, he believes just the opposite to be true. He suggests that they fail because of *too much* capital, which allows them to solve problems with money instead of creativity, and so in the end, they often have the same problems and less money. This philosophy suited me just fine, in that it sounded like the creative, lazy poor man's approach. Back then, I wouldn't have known where to start to raise more money, and money has always scared me anyway. I have only recently learned anything meaningful about it. The truth is, I have never balanced my own personal checkbook, and I still don't know how it's done. I have held to Hawken's idea, maybe to my detriment, by not recognizing the need for cash sometimes, but all's well that ends well (so far).

In Petaluma we began to host our "Thursday night free beer tasting open houses" after work and right in the brewery. That lasted for years and got us in all sorts of minor, and later major, trouble. We were also growing very fast and jumping into projects without first getting permits, which made for a less-than-excellent relationship with the city's planning department. The truth was that I often didn't know we would need certain things until it was too late, and I had to fill the gap quickly. Things like putting up a malt silo without getting a permit, or putting a refrigeration unit on the roof without calling the landlord first, routing out a floor drain, adding electrical circuits, stuff like that.

Our initial 1994 use permit with the City of Petaluma was a pretty straightforward affair. What took six or seven months in Forest Knolls took about six weeks in Petaluma. That was a big deal because, as you remember, we had to relocate quick-like. But that would be the last time things were easy with the planning department. I'll start at the end, because only there was the stink put where it belonged. The city is always a big part of your brewery, whereas if you're in the stationery business or in the screw-machine business, well, nobody cares much. Alcohol can bring out the best and worst in people, and it is amazing how much the future of your experience of running your business can be influenced by invisible individuals working against you. The ones who are inclined to help you mostly do so by staying out of the way in regulatory situations. They allow you to move through the system easily and with good intentions. But if somebody in a bureaucracy wants to impede you, they can be hard to recognize.

So we'll blast forward way down the road to the summer of 2004, when we received a letter from the City Water Delivery Department's general manager telling us that water service would be interrupted for a couple of days in the near future. I called to learn about the details, because it seemed like it might disrupt production, and I ended up speaking to the GM, who sounded very cool. He said he wanted to come to the brewery and talk about it, and was sure he could make it work out for us. He said he wanted to come to the plant just because he hadn't seen it since we had moved there. I had become used to the city department guys treating us as though we were a problem.

When he showed up for the appointment we made, I was in my office noodling on my guitar. It happened to be in open G tuning—a.k.a. slack-key tuning, or Hawaiian tuning. The guy walked in, and he was a big soft-spoken Samoan guy. He told me that he grew up in Hawaii and had learned to play traditional hulas from a very old man who lived way up the mountain. So I handed him the guitar and, unbelievably, he was a master of Hawaiian slack-key.

He played so easily; it was really beautiful. Well, we became instant friends, and I was an admirer, because that sound is very delicate and tricky to do well. It takes discipline. Coincidentally (are there really any coincidences?), I had been spending the previous several years learning to play traditional finger-style guitar blues from the Piedmont area of the Carolinas, which has its own very serious dogma. We talked guitar. We talked very little about the water shutoff, because before he came to see me he'd already rescheduled the work for the middle of the night on a weekend so it wouldn't affect us. I offered to offset the OT for his crew, but he declined, saying, "It's cool." I didn't know what to say. He told me he was a big fan of our beer and had been to our original free-beer Thursday open-house parties. I told him he looked familiar, which he did, and asked why he'd never introduced himself, seeing as we were doing everything we did with *his* water. He just said quietly that he liked visiting the brewery scene and didn't wanna make a big deal out of it. It is good to have friends.

My experience with the city hadn't usually included that sort of kindness (although over the last few years we have found beer lovers hiding in some very important corners in the corpus of the city offices). I thanked him and listened to some more slack-key hula, and I asked him if he had ever worked with the city planner we had been dealing with. He looked at me and rolled his eyes and said, "She sure has got it in for you." Huh? "Yep," he said. He told me how she had once e-mailed him asking for a letter stating that "Lagunitas's continued growth should be constrained because its water use will place a strain on the City Water Delivery Department's ability to provide water for the whole city in the future." I asked him how he responded, and he said he told her "No." She pressed him more, but he told her he wouldn't because "It's just not the truth." I thanked him profusely and took him on the nicest and most casual tour of the brewery ever, and then offered to pay off the mortgage on his house and to get him an Enzo Ferrari.

The city council—the political body—always seemed to like and support us in the community because we were involved with nonprofit-group donations, and the city council members were on the boards of most of those groups. We never worked directly with the city council, though, because our interaction with the city was mostly permit stuff, which is very bureaucratic. The planner who handled our permits eventually squared off against us in some very unprofessional ways (even in light of our history), and we called in the big guns. The political element set things straight for us, and we have been good campers ever since. Considering how fast we were moving and how short on resources like time and money we were, I think it would have been hard to have done much better.

In the years since we first got up and going in Petaluma, the planner assigned to alcoholic beverage licensees has stood in our way over all kinds of permit applications and use permit–modification requests, including bottling, getting malt in a silo, doing tastings, selling kegs, doing tours, managing our wastewater, having events at the brewery, moving to the McDowell brewery, adding outdoor tanks, having a shed over our outdoor air compressor, keeping unused equipment out back, eliminating parking spaces, adding parking spaces, expanding our premises, you name it. One time, over a permit for an event, she told one of my good guys to "sign here while you look me in the eye and say you'll have at least ten guys working security, even though I know you are lying."

He didn't sign, and we did have the security needed, and the event went ahead and all was well, but only because the mayor became involved. The next part was a lesson in pure politics. Early one morning I called the mayor's office and in reluctant tones described the intense and compromising difficulties I had been enduring with respect to the Planning and Use Permit process. I apologized for calling but was at my wit's end and was only looking for a little guidance as to how I could address the problem within the city's management structure.

Throwing someone under the bus incorrectly can have drastic consequences and blowback. I reminded myself that there is never, ever a long-term downside to speaking truth to power. The mayor was surprisingly sympathetic and said he would call the offending party's supervisor right away, and that I should call him the next day and make an appointment to meet with both of them. In the course of the conversation, I told the mayor that the planner and the waste-water guy were coming with some others that very morning to do a walk-through. They had given no particular reason, just a by-then ritual hunting expedition. The wastewater guy, in fact, told me, "I am an enforcement officer; I don't even need to ask permission to walk through your plant." That wastoid would sometimes come around to the back of the building, enter through the brew house, and ask the brewers how much beer they were making, thinking that he would get a more honest answer from them than from me. It freaked out the brewers and was creepy. I finally wrote his supervisor and stated that while I recognized his authority to perform unannounced inspections, he must still come to the front office and obtain an escort, because the brewery was a dangerous place. They respected my request going forward. The wastewater guy was a strangely duplicitous piece of work, and in time he would also be flushed from the scene, but let's keep it to one creep at a time.

So the planner would be there at 10:30 AM, and the mayor told me that he'd come by a little early—around 10:00 AM—and maybe I could show him around the brewery first. The planner and the waste-water guy both pulled up promptly at 10:30, just as the mayor and I walked out a door at the other end of the building and into the parking lot across the way, where the planner and her henchmen could see us from a distance. The mayor stopped me and said, "Let's stand here and pretend to talk casually." He gestured large and laughed at something I didn't even say. The planner and wastewater guy looked over as our imaginary conversation continued. The mayor waved to them from across the lot, and we walked briskly over to them. The mayor greeted the planner warmly, but she looked more than a little ill at ease. The wastewater guy tried to be invisible.

I'll never know exactly what the subtext was, but beginning the very next week, the planner became a rubber stamp for everything we wanted. At some point down the road I went into the planning department and asked for her, and the counter person told me that she had resigned—and then smiled. I couldn't restrain myself, and I pronounced a pregnant "Reeeallly?" I asked where she'd gone, and the woman said, "I can't say, but whatever you do, don't open a business in Napa County." That was useful advice! It turned out that the mayor too, appropriately, was on the board of many of the same Petaluma nonprofit organizations we'd been donating to for years. It's good to have friends. The wastewater guy lasted a couple of months and finally left to take a job at the Wastewater Department in a city to the north. I have heard from local breweries up there that he is as he was.

When I think of these city department folks, I am reminded of Carlos Castaneda's petty tyrants. They were that. And I learned what I had to learn from them.

Now, rewind back to 1997, when we were still in our first diminutive Petaluma roost and growing quickly. It was all I could do to pay the ordinary bills, and it was very difficult and equally expensive to borrow money to buy new equipment, but I knew we were overworking the space we were in and had to find some money somehow so we could move into a bigger and more purpose-built space.

I wondered about a joint venture of some kind, and went over to the now-defunct Golden Pacific Brewing Co. in Berkeley to see if there might be any interest in letting us co-use their new and so-far-underutilized plant. I did the same with the also-now-defunct Sonoma Mountain Brewery. Nothing came of either thing. Both of those brands had built very nice and well-equipped production breweries, but their brands were flagging in the harsh environment of enormous industry-wide 1997 overcapacity. I had a brand that was working really well, and a seriously crummy and inefficient plant, so it had seemed like a good match, had they been so inclined.

But hope springs eternal, and their fates were sealed. Both thought that what we were accomplishing was either lucky or easy. They both saw craft brewing as a market, with a capital *M*. They could gauge its metrics, research its demographics, solve its formulae, and deliver a liquid solution that would answer a specific reservoir of unfulfilled demand. There is still a lot of this thinking around. This is mostly Big Brewery thinking. Even a big craft brewer is still small in the context of the genuinely big. As we get bigger, I am trying harder and harder to think smaller and smaller. Ironic what works sometimes.

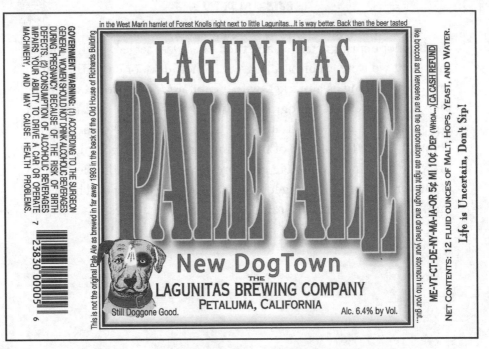

Still Doggone Good.

New DogTown

THE
LAGUNITAS BREWING COMPANY
PETALUMA, CALIFORNIA

Alc. 6.4% by Vol.

in the West Marin hamlet of Forest Knolls right next to little Lagunitas...It is way better. Back then the beer tasted

like broccoli and kerosene and the carbonation ate right through and drained your stomach into your gut...

This is not the original Pale Ale as brewed in far away 1993 in the back of the Old House of Richards Building.

ME-VT-CT-DE-NY-MA-IA-OR 5¢ MI 10¢ DEP (WHOA...) CA CASH REFUND

NET CONTENTS: 12 FLUID OUNCES OF MALT, HOPS, YEAST, AND WATER.

Life is Uncertain, Don't Sip!

First Brewed in April, 2009

There's an old saying; 'The more things change, the more they change'. This is NOT the same tasty Pale Ale we brewed at the beginning. It has accomplished what we all eventually want for ourselves; It has been made new again. We never let this sexy old girl go unbrewed... We dug its hops and its soft malt thing, but as we at the Brewery have changed we, well, we grew apart. So we decided to get her a chin lift. The results were good, we got a tummy tuck and a brow flip to go with it and there was a little flab that we lipo-sucked out. The results were so good that we went all the way and performed a scalp-scrape, a through-the-arm-pit implant thingy, a toe flop, a cuticle float, a radical corto-conical inter-abdominal spine snip and hip and knuckle replacement to boot. Now the beer is almost unrecognizable even to its former self and while the final version is brighter and more sexy in every way, the same old girl is still underneath it all in the soul of the flavor as it spreads itself across your palate and enters your blood on its way to your brain to make your mind do tricks... Give us a call sometime! 707-769-4495

14

MOVING AGAIN

*I*t was a bad time for the craft brew industry in 1997. Because of that, I thought that it would be hard to raise the money needed to move into a new building. And it *was* hard. Since it seemed like there was so much underused brewing capacity already installed in the area, I worried that I shouldn't be sticking my neck out so far. The bigger and stupid suicidal Oregon and Washington breweries were driving six-pack prices down routinely to $4.99, and Henry Weinhard's was successfully posing as a micro and selling $4.99 twelve-packs.

I can remember the big introduction of Weinhard's Raspberry Hefeweizen beer and even Old Milwaukee Red. All were very cheap, and in those earlier days it was more than a little confusing to most craft-beer fans. On top of all that, there were new craft-beer brands appearing in the San Francisco market every couple of days. It was a blur for everyone. The world was a mess all around us. Nice time for pricing if you were a consumer, but tough to run a business on. A bunch of the breweries doing the crazy pricing had gone public, and so they had big bank accounts and probably figured that some sort of war of attrition was going to occur, and when it was over, and they were the last brands standing, they'd clean up. One time back then, while walking my dog around the block and pondering the enormity of the money I was starting to owe, I counted twenty-three serious brands that had only recently been important brewers and were suddenly gone from the market. There was beer running in the streets. Distributors started getting tired of all the brands, retailers were just numb, and beer fans were more than a little bowled over. But it was also a good time to be buying used equipment, for the same reasons.

The list of breweries that disappeared is a long one. Who remembers San Rafael Ales, Golden Pacific, Sonoma Mountain Brewing, Heckler Brau, Jet City Brewing, Nor'Wester Brewing Company, Arcata Brewing, Pacific Hop Exchange, Hart Brewing, Big Trees Brewing Co., Carmel Brewing, Apollo Brewing, Hangtown Brewing, Saxer Brewing Company, Napa Ale Works, Mermaid Brewing, Devil Mountain Brewing Company, Rhino Chasers, Thomas Kemper, Umpqua Brewing Company, Wizard Brewing, Lake Tahoe Brewing? It's a long list, and those are just the names I can remember from our little local slice of the national pie.

We finally worked out our plan to raise the money from the friends and friends-of-friends network, locked in a new building across the street from our current location in Petaluma, and started doing the engineering and construction and grave robbing of used equipment. We bought a lot of gear from the Wisconsin Brewing Co.: one thirty-barrel brew house and three fermenters, a bottling tank, stainless sinks, and miscellaneous other stuff. They'd built their brewery on the shores of the Wisconsin River just above the one-hundred-year flood line, then promptly got flooded out two years in a row. They weren't making it go anyway, so they pulled the plug. We bought the Napa Ale Works plant and landed a big fermenter and a boiler and a bottling tank and lots of other useful stuff. There is a lot of "stuff" in the brewing business. We un-sweated absolutely all of their copper pipe and cut up their steam piping, reusing it all eventually. That brewery was owned by a smart guy who'd worked for the old Anderson Consulting firm, and he founded a big sparkling-wine operation for some even bigger French folk. However, success in wine does not seem to be very transferrable to craft beer. Beer people and wine people are like cat people versus dog people, Beatles versus Elvis, Alice versus Trixie, Betty versus Veronica. You just gotta choose. It's hard to be both.

The people who owned Carmel Brewing had other interests in the farmworker Porta Potti business (yum), and the brewery was not thriving like their honey-wagon project, so they sold their brand to a Bangalore-based global brewery pirate who was trying to scoop up brands and make a big business out of a bunch of smaller ones. He was a billionaire, so I guess that made him think that he was smart enough to do it. But for us, the closing of the Carmel production plant yielded a complete bottling line, several fermenters (recently sold to the crazy-cool people at Three Floyds Brewing), and a bottling tank. That was how it was then. Kegs, tanks, keg fillers, more fermenters, even sinks and lab equipment. It was for sale on every street corner, and it was pretty darn cheap. I recently sold some of that stuff for a little more than I paid for it, and it was still a good price for the buyer. How many things that you use actually appreciate in value? But it was all a fire sale back then. However, all the bad news in the industry made banks nervous. The stuff was cheap, but the money to get it was expensive. It seems most things work out to be a zero-sum game, or maybe the "house" always has its 2 percent advantage.

While we were still brewing away in our Ross Street brewery, we were doing the demolition work on the new building's old six-inch concrete floor slab and preparing the crummy expansive clay soil underneath for the new floor-drain plumbing and the twenty-four inches of concrete and steel that would withstand a 7.0 earthquake while supporting the two million pounds of tanks and brewery equipment that we wouldn't even have for another seven years.

Money was going to be tight for the move into the new facility, in part because I had never done anything like that before, and to make a hard job harder, the decision to do it once again came pretty quickly. We decided how much money we could raise would be limited by a balance between the guesstimated value of the business and my absolute intention of maintaining ownership control. The only thing I knew for sure was that we needed to revamp our situation. One option would have been to seriously carve up our existing space and install floor drains everywhere, then raise parts of the roof and bring in more electricity. The list of major renovation projects was going to be very long. Or we could look for another space to move to where we could build out to spec while we continued to make beer where we were. Either way, the decision had to be made in the space of a couple months, because I was already raising the money that we would need one way or the other. The stars aligned, as they so often did, and I found a perfect spot almost across the street. The landlord knew the brand and liked it, and was willing to invest and even put up a big part of the improvements cost (we would pay it back during the course of a five-year lease). We went to work.

The new brew house and all the other scrounged gear was on its way, and I selected a contractor to do the extensive concrete work. All my ducks were in perfect little rows. In the realm of things that make you go "Huh?" one week into tearing all the existing concrete floors out of the seventeen-thousand-square-foot building, I got a call from the contractor's estimator saying that he needed to increase his estimate by about 25 percent. I laughed out loud at first, because my budget had already been set in a different sort of concrete, and then I realized I was laughing alone. There was a long silence on the phone, and he waited for me to restart the conversation. Taking the bait, I said, "Reeeealllly?" He told me that he'd forgotten to include the labor. I took a deep breath, assumed a lotus position, then a Drunken Eagle, inhaled white sage smoke, and regained my composure with a flawless Pooping Crane while being administered smelling salts. I leaned forward and repeated my earlier question, to which he said, "Yes, reeee-alllly." There wasn't much to do; he was a good guy and probably in trouble with his boss. The work had already begun, and, well, whatever.

That was the first of many cost overruns. Like being nibbled to death by ducks, no one nibble hurt very much, but they added up. In the words of my investor/landlord, "It's like a monkey standing on the cash register pissing. [pause for effect] It runs into the money." I have no idea where that expression comes from, but it is a strange image, and it is true. We poured the concrete, did the plumbing, fixed up the electrical, bought all this other used stuff, moved into the new McDowell brewery, and got to work. It was a crazy, high-mileage time for me and my liver and my wife. But the brand was still growing well, people were digging what we were doing, and with new labels, names, and recipes, we were having fun breaking the rules and making up new ones.

This is probably more common than I know, but the way we executed the move to the new brewery was a sort of a dovetailed-joint process. Once the new concrete floors were in place, we installed the new fermenters and bright beer tanks and the boiler and the cooling systems. We got the new tanks ready to fill. I'd bought a larger brew house (thirty barrels), but I didn't want to brew with it for a while. I'd seen a lot of the established beer companies build new breweries—some very, very elaborate—but when they began to brew in them, the beers changed, and almost never for the better. It was the kind of thing that a lot of people noticed and talked about. This was often a disaster, because the only reason to open a new brewery was to make more beer, but when the beer changed as a result, sales often slumped and the waters got choppy really fast. This scenario was happening all around us, and I wanted to think of a way to manage the change. The public-opinion thing mattered a lot, and sometimes it was unfair, but it was real. So I decided we'd brew with our old brew house (fourteen barrels) for the first six months or so, and then phase in the new brew house later. That way, we'd make the beer exactly the same way and we'd get past that particular bridge before bringing the new brew house on-line. It worked out pretty well, but it made for a tricky move into the new building, which went like this:

When the new brewery's basic infrastructure was in place, we brewed like crazy in the old one, filling every tank in the old brewery with fermenting or finished beer. Then, one Friday night in January 1999, we unplugged the old brew house after the last tank was filled at 10:00 PM and began moving it over to the new building. The old brewery would continue to bottle the beer that was cued up all the way back to the fermenters. We installed the old brew house in the new building by the following Tuesday morning and immediately began brewing there, filling the new fermenters we had just bought. The old bottling line slowly emptied the tanks in the old brewery, and we shipped from there. As soon as the first beer went into tanks at the new brewery, we knew we had fourteen days to get the bottling tanks hooked up and the new bottling line assembled so that we could keep bottling going as the old brewery went dry. Each day, when we emptied a fermentation tank at the old brewery, we loaded it onto a truck and drove it to the new brewery and filled it again. It was like turning a reversible sock inside out. Think about it, you'll see it.

When we had the new place mostly ready, we had a big moving party, inviting twelve hundred or so of our best friends, and after a ten-brewery tasting and some live music while getting loaded at the old plant, a loud horn blew, everybody grabbed anything they could carry that was not nailed down, and we all marched over to the new McDowell plant in a massive parade led by a mime, a guy on stilts, a purple bear, and a tragic little Civil War–style marching band. The passing parade stopped traffic on McDowell Boulevard for about twenty minutes. The purple bear and the guy on stilts assumed traffic-cop duties. The city cops were supposed to be there to make the crosswalk, but mistakes had been made, and the parade had left the station. In the new brewery, a rockin' blues band was already hard into a shuffle beat as all twelve hundred of us marched in, poured into the expansive and as-yet mostly empty brewery, and the future was born.

Over the next few years, there was still a lot of good equipment for sale, and I grabbed every tank I could find. We bought a really nice ninety-barrel tank from Pyramid Breweries when they closed their old Kalima, Washington, plant. We bought their old reefer plant too, and it is still running strong today. It turned out that the ninety-barrel Kalima tank was a little too big to get in the building. The brewers named it Holmes, after John Holmes, because it was too big to fit inside. But we took the liberty of modifying it in ways John Holmes never would have allowed. We bought a big tank destined for a brewery that closed before the tanks were even finished! Later, we also had two new 120-barrel tanks built by JV Northwest, and then two more by John Cross that also turned out to be too tall to get in, but I didn't know that before I started the daylong process of trying.

Those 120-barrel tanks accidentally were built six inches taller than the drawings, but we didn't notice that until it was too late. We went through our usual mini-Egyptian process for getting them in horizontally through a door that was six inches wider than the tank lying down. Then, as they got through the door, we slowly tilted them into a vertical standing position. That was when we noticed that they were too tall. It had taken me five or six hours to get them to that point, only to discover the extra six inches. If you can picture it, when you stand a tank up there is a moment, at sixty degrees, where it is taller than it will be when standing all the way up. At that critical too-tall moment, the tank bound up tight between the floor and the ceiling's two-by-eight beams.

I was not going backward. The legs for those tanks are all engineered for seismic zone four (the toughest earthquake-proof engineering), so the base is a very rigid structure with big diagonal braces. I got onto a forklift and (gently at first, then less so) rammed the forklift against the legs, levering the tank upward against the ceiling in a full-throttle 7.2 seismic event, while the tank top, which was bound against the ceiling joists, lifted the entire roof up a few inches. Finally, the tank stood up and the roof settled back down. I waited for a moment, sitting in the forklift cage, to see if the ceiling would stay put, and it did. While I was ramming the legs with the forklift, all of my brewers were watching in what looked like genuine fear. They were crouching under adjacent tanks, eyeing the doors. There were two of the tanks to get in that way, and for me it was invigorating. I'm ten years older now, with an enhanced sense of my own mortality, and I don't think I could bring myself to do something like that anymore. But it worked.

There was very little careful planning during that time. I had the picture crisp in my mind, but I was always a little loose about the details. Sometimes inviting chance in that way has huge benefits, sometimes not.

It was 1999, and while we had been able to stay above all the poop piling up around most of the rest of the industry, it's hard to be in the world without getting a little bit on you. We continued to grow at 23 percent year over year, but it was the slowest growth we had seen, and it was a time when we really needed to grow quickly because of all of our new debt and overhead. Even though we were using the old brew house for flavor continuity, we were having some stability issues due to the old/new bottling line's age and the resultant oxygen pickup by the beer during bottling—meaning that if the beer hung around for a couple of months in the pipeline on the way to being sold, it could end up tasting stale. Yuck. Timing, timing, timing. That was the start of the very hardest of the hard cash years, and my brewers and bottlers had to do even more with minimal production upgrades.

In 2000 we bought a used keg-filling line from another casualty of the late 1990s crunch, Spanish Peaks Brewing Co. (which has since reopened). The guy who built it lived up in Canada. His experience of building this one-of-a-kind piece of equipment was so financially devastating that he would no longer help with repairs unless we flew him down first class, and then he'd still be argumentative and unhappy. We've been pretty much on our own with it to this day, but to his credit, it has been amazingly reliable. It has filled thirty kegs an hour for us since the first day we fired it up, and it was retired in January 2010 when we installed our newest used keg line, bought from Summit Brewing in Minnesota. I expect it to fill more than sixty-three kegs every hour for the next ten years. The old keg line also went to Three Floyds. I hope it serves them as well as it did us.

We ran the plant frugally while only adding tanks and kegs and stuff to allow us eventually to get the thirty-barrel brew house running at almost full speed. After five years, we were finally paying off all the stuff we had bought to get into the building. That meant we could start all over again. The first thing that had to go was the bottling line. It was crushing us to be running it so hard and to be wasting so much beer in the process.

As I described earlier, in 2003 we began plans to replace it. That was a big deal from a financing and operational standpoint. Our old filler was so terribly inefficient that we wasted 5 to 8 percent of the beer that went into it every day. This wasting came in the form of short-filled bottles, bent caps, broken bottles, and other things that wasted the finished beer after it was in the glass. That is a bigger dollar-value number than you think. If that beer had instead survived the filler and gotten into bottles and onto pallets and into trucks to be sold, the additional money from those sales would have made the monthly payment four times over on a brand-new, shiny, still-in-the-wrapper, $1 million, Italian-built, depalletizer-unscrambler-rinser-filler-crowner machine with new bottle conveyors and a drop-packer and case sealer. That meant that we, in a way of thinking, would get the whole filling line for free. I guess it is sorta like hitting yourself in the head with a hammer: if you do it long enough, it just feels so good when you stop. When the new line was finally in and all the Italians left and the brand-new machine was up and running, the plant was a whole other place. It looked nice, it sounded nice, it ran nice without breaking down every other day the way our previous forty-four-year-old filler had, it treated the beer nice, it was nice for the bottling-line guys, it made us nice and profitable, and for the first time in thirteen years, everything was nice. For the sake of comparison, the filler alone could be traded for a very nice condition Jaguar XJ220. Nice.

This was about the time a handful of the other mid-1990s generation of breweries began to rebuild their plants too. Some breweries with deeper pockets built entirely new buildings, but Sonoma County was a very expensive real-estate market, and given our dicey financial past, I had to be very careful, even paranoid. They say that a cat that likes to sit on a hot stove won't sit on a cold one, and I'm that kind of cat. Instead, we rebuilt it all in place. It was like performing surgery on an awake and argumentative patient, but every day was like Christmas for a few years.

When we considered the available suppliers for the new bottling line, we called the old guard of bottle-filler companies. They all came in to make initial presentations, but it was pretty clear that none of them would be taking our cute little brewery all that seriously. These were global companies accustomed to accepting *big* orders from the *big* brewers and *big* soda companies. Sitting in our crowded and noisy office and talking about a million dollars of equipment while being bumped by people on their way to the bathroom after tours probably seemed a little hokey, but that was what we were.

We found a less-well-known bottle-filler builder from Italy that was trying to remake its reputation in the United States. The Italians

made good still wine fillers, but they had a spotty reputation for support and spare parts and such. The representative worked hard to convince me that they were newly committed to the US market. They felt
that if they could sell us one, then they could use us as a showroom. I
had a friend whom this company was also trying to recruit as a second
US sales rep, and he hipped me to their pricing structure. Using that
good inside info, I was able to get a ripping price on great equipment,
and since then, they have sold at least four other fillers to our peers
in the area. The whole thing was a win-win for all of us. They wanted
the same thing we wanted: to build their business and establish their
reputation. I used this same modus operandi in choosing our suppliers for all of our subsequent upgrades, and it has worked out well. We
have real partners.

Once the filler was doing its job and making us some extra cash,
we began to work our way upstream into the brewery. We upgraded
our filtration department with a totally state-of-the-art Alfa Laval
Centrifuge separator. The thing looked and sounded like it belonged
in a NASA lab. Our old filter system was OK, but it could only run
about a half a barrel per minute, and it was very often plugged up by
the increasing volume of beer we were moving through it. Sometimes
a filtration would go poorly and the filter guy would end up working
an eighteen-hour shift, napping in the Beer Loft while the beer eked its
way through the filter all night long. That had been going on forever
in the filtration department, and it sucked. I had done my share of
time on that watch in the past. The new centrifuge would change the
filtration work forever.

Not only would the thing work better and sound better, but a
high-speed centrifuge filtration system could clarify the thicker
yeasty-paste beer further down in the fermenter. This was yeast
that was full of beer that we used to have to pump out to the drain,
because it was way too thick for our old filter to handle. If you've ever
home-brewed, you know what I'm talking about. It's that last hazy
beer in the carboy that sits on top of the yeast just as the siphon stops
siphoning. In the glass carboy it may be about one twenty-two-ounce
bottle that gets left behind, but in a big 120-barrel fermenter it is about

three to five whole barrels of beer. In a three-hundred-barrel tank, it's more like five to eight barrels. Cha-ching! In any case, dumping all that perfectly good but unobtainable beer was a very serious form of alcohol abuse!

We bought the cool new system (with the new profitability from the bottle-filling line) to clarify the beer. It looked nice, it sounded nice, and it ran nice without plugging up every day like our old filter system. It treated the beer nice, it was nice for the filter guys, it filtered one whole barrel every minute, and it made us even more nice and profitable. All of that beer had been extremely flavorful wastewater before, and suddenly it was going into bottles on its way to the bank. Everything was nice. In 2010 we replaced *that* cool system with a bigger, badder, and even-more-intense-in-every-way centrifuge that currently moves two barrels per minute. It never ends.

There is a little bit more to the buying of the new centrifuge. See, the company that built the machine has a great reputation for quality and service. The first, smaller machine that we bought from them seriously tested that reputation. From almost the day that it was commissioned, we had troubles with it. Problems of oxygen pickup (very bad for the beer) and machine vibrations. These centrifuges are actually pretty scary machines when you think of what can go wrong with them. Check this out: inside of the centrifuge there is a stainless-steel, two-foot thick, twenty-five-hundred-pound bowl spinning at five thousand rpm. A circle with a diameter of two feet has a circumference of about 6'4". If the thing is going round five thousand times per minute, that is about eighty-three times per second. That means that the twenty-five-hundred-pound hunk of stainless is moving at 523 feet per second—or 357 miles per hour—inside of the building, with an operator standing three feet away. That is more than a ton of stainless steel going around in tiny circles four feet from your face at half the speed of sound. Think of it in terms of momentum: if the bowl was coming at you in a straight line with all that energy, it would seem to weigh 895,000 pounds, or at least it would take an 895,000-pound stationary mass to stop it. I'm not sure all the concrete in the whole brewery weighs 895,000 pounds.

When we turn the machine off in normal operation, it takes the better part of an hour for the bowl to stop spinning, even with the braking mechanism engaged.

There is a research video that is rumored to exist where the machine maker put one of these beasts into a reinforced concrete bunker and loaded it so that a vibration was induced that caused the twenty-five-hundred-pound bowl to vibrate wildly enough to break loose from the bearing it spins upon. The story is that the stainless bowl got hot, then it got hotter, then it glowed red, then it melted, flinging molten metal and other pieces of itself right through the walls of the concrete bunker that encased it. At some point the camera stopped working.

The machine we had was vibrating. Vibrations are measured in millimeters per second, and 11mm/sec is a lot. Again, imagine that 895,000-pound mass coming off its bearing toward your face. Frequently it would vibrate enough so that the machine's internal software would trigger an emergency shutdown and the e-brake would come on and the machine would go limp in about an hour! I can only guess that they picked the limit of vibration based on the vibration experiment in that concrete test bunker. When the thing would have one of its fits, if it didn't shut itself down, the brewers who operated it would hit the shutdown button and then exit the building and have lunch five or six blocks away from the centrifuge.

The company that built it was always there to work on it and tried for months and months to figure out why the thing was vibrating like it was. They really were on the case, but in the end it just seemed like a lemon situation. Nobody knew why; it just was. I was able to convince the company to take it back if we would promise to buy a new and larger machine. They gave us credit for the full value of the old one toward the new one, and gave us a great discount on the new one as well. We had been a good showroom for them, and when other brewers would visit to "shop" the machine, we always kept the problems mum to support our partner. It worked out well for both of us. For the record, the new machine runs great and costs about the same as a clean, low-mileage 2009 Ferrari F50.

As time went along, the once-huge thirty-barrel-brew-house schedule expanded to seven brews per day, twenty-four hours a day, seven days a week, and its time had come. The next step was to use the profitability from the extra beer the centrifuge could liberate to pay for a new, fully automated brew house. Just like with the bottling line, we called the big guys in the business. They came, they saw, they looked at us and snickered, and we never called them back. The guys we picked instead were pirates, like ourselves, and they built a very sleek and totally state-of-the-art system for us. It was designed and built in Bavaria by real Bavarians—the best in the world at that sort of engineering. The guys who owned the company were younger guys and had started it just a few years earlier. They had all worked for the big and established brew-house builders before, and had jumped ship to do their own thing. I knew they wanted what I wanted: to make a good reputation for themselves, pay their rent, buy groceries for their kids, and build a company. They had already built three other brew houses for other craft guys our size, but ours would be the most technically sophisticated system yet.

When other brewers expanded their brew houses, most just built a new addition onto their buildings or built whole new locations, but Sonoma County real estate was some of the most expensive in the world, and I couldn't see how we could make that happen. Once again, we had to do it all in place while keeping the old brew house running, open-heart-surgery-style. Our portion of the project began in earnest eight months before the brew house even left Germany. This installation, more so than any other to date, required upgrading every system that supplied every utility to the brewery: water, electrical power, our natural gas supply. We increased our city water supply to a three-inch main. We replaced the building's four hundred amps of 220-volt three-phase power with an additional one thousand amps of full-on scary 480-volt power. We increased the size of our meter for our natural gas supply and put in a four-inch supply line all the way to the back of the brewery. The natural gas meter is on the outside wall that my desk used to be up against. When everything was running, I could actually hear the gas meter whirring through the wall.

Like those little puzzles where you have to get all the numbers in sequence by sliding the squares around one at a time, so it was with the scheme to install the new brew house. We could not stop brewing for a few moments, let alone for a few months, so we prepared a new spot twenty feet north of the existing brew house's location to move that old brew house into temporarily. We'd install the new brew house and then disassemble the old one, and later that spot would house our expanded keg line, and even that would be temporary. We installed a big removable skylight over the brew house so that the nine new vessels could be dropped in quickly without having to resort to our customary Egyptian tip-em-up methodology. Glycol lines were redeployed; floors were epoxied; walls were built; natural gas, electrical systems, water, steam, compressed air, and CO_2 gas systems were stubbed in; and seven years of accumulated black mold was excised from the walls and ceiling with scrapers, grinders, and raw bleach. A shiny new 1.21 gigawatt high-pressure gas boiler was installed, along with a carbon water-filtration system and a mondo tank of potassium hydroxide (stuff that dissolves organic material—like you and me). Our liquid CO_2 tank morphed from three tons to six. We extended our old malt silo by twenty thousand pounds of capacity and brought in a second one as well. Everything got badder.

As we had done eight years before, one Friday afternoon in December we pulled the big plug and, over the course of ninety-six hours, moved our existing brew house twenty feet to its temporary location (where it too had pre-stubbed-in utilities of every type awaiting its arrival) so that we could install the new one over the course of what we thought would be three months. In the end, the installation ended up taking more than eight months.

The vessels and equipment all arrived in a convoy of lowboys, flatbeds, and drayage trucks transferred off of a container ship that—having left the port of Bremen, Germany, and passed through the Panama Canal and survived a bunch of huge Pacific storms that even dented the mash tun and the kettle on the top—arrived at the brewery right on time. We got out the crowbars. The monster crane rig arrived to unload and place the very sexiest kinds of new gear. It removed the skylight like the lid on a can of sardines and spent the next ten hours delicately grasping the vessels, raising them to the sky, and lowering them through the new hole, seeding the waiting brew-house area with the elements of its future self.

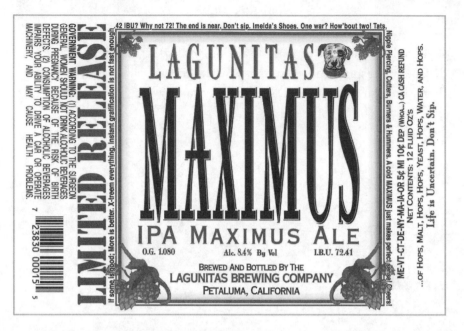

First Brewed in January, 1995

*B*ig beers are good and Big IPA's are even better. But it's kind'a like, well, first you ride some great wheelies and then you get it in your head to try jumping stuff. Maybe you start with a ramp in the driveway and then you move on to bigger things like a real cougar and rattle snakes. It's a rush and all your freinds think you're pretty cool, but eventually even that's not enough so you jump through fire, some trucks, some Dodge's, some Semi's, a fountain, and later a pile of wrecked cars. While making strong beers it's hard to screw the pooch and end up steppin' off into a rag doll boogie, but your taste buds got a little twisted and over time you start to think that only bigger is better. Eventually you try to jump your beer over the Snake Canyon and end up in the river with a headache. We do dig our beers big and we do dig an occasional No-Handed Can-Can, a solid McMetz, or a Superman S-Grab... but balance is still the most important skill of all and the MAXIMUS IPA is exactly that. Ride it. Taste the hops. Slurp the malt. Drink the juice! Live to see another day...

A WORD ABOUT BREWERS

THE GHOSTS IN THE MACHINES

Even a modest brew house is still a complex system intended to flow raw materials in one end and coherently flow a rich and delicious broth (wort) out of the other. In the case of our old brew house, the brewer was the artisan, the ghost in the machine. He facilitated every nuanced operation through the performance of a carefully learned dance that lasts eight hours and has no repeating steps, like an old shamanic ritual. Our newest brewers would arrive as ordinarily healthy people on day one, but after a few months of working at Lagunitas, I have seen brewer after brewer begin to stand taller, look leaner, lose twenty pounds, become buff, and take up free-climbing rock faces and single-speed mountain-bike racing. Brewing is pretty different in every brewery because of the level of tribal knowledge that has to be passed on from brewer to brewer as the business grows and people come and go. And like tribal lore, legends evolve and myths accumulate. The brewing process becomes a form of sacred knowledge that is passed on, but with some level of variation. This can be good or it can be bad. It has the potential to optimize institutional knowledge and select for efficiency, but every now and then some level of operational genetic drift is introduced and all hell breaks loose, as hell is wont to do.

Hell paid us a visit back in about 2000 when I accidentally hired a guy whose destiny eventually lay with the city sewer company, but not

151

until he had turned our brewery into a bit of the same. He presented himself as a lab manager but would mostly spend his time grokking some really bent porn magazines while unknowingly mixing seriously undisciplined wild yeast in with our own precious and previously monocultural brewing yeast.

Nature, as we all figure out eventually, has a pretty active imagination. I mean, c'mon . . . 358 varieties of parrots? Nipples on men? A billion varieties of wild yeast? Yeasts that ferment sugar, yeasts that ferment iron, yeasts that ferment alcohol, yeasts that ferment what other yeasts cannot. There are yeast cells absolutely everywhere in the world. Under a cactus's needles in Patagonia. On a stone in the Antarctic. A brewery is all about total control of nature, and diversity is anathema. Microcultural yeast diversity has no place in most breweries. Some very old European and some very new American breweries work in uneasy relationships with that diversity, and some do it successfully, but as a rule, brewing is the definition of monoculture. As I mentioned earlier, in any one of our thirty-some fermentation tanks there are about thirty quadrillion yeast cells, all identical, all clones of each other, all happily pooping out CO_2 and ethanol while living their yeasty little single-celled lives, munching contentedly on luscious short-chain malt sugars prepared especially for them.

Along with bottling lines and centrifuges and brew houses, a key but invisible piece of human-inhabited equipment in a brewery is its lab. This is usually one of the last things to get seriously upgraded, and usually only after it is already needed—or at least that was the way it was for us. All the horses out of the barn? OK, then close the door.

The wild-yeast thing resulted in no bad beer flavors, which was a fabulous accident of yeasty genetics, but instead it made beer that badly wanted out of the bottle. The comments we received about this were all surprisingly friendly. It was very cool that most who wrote or called assumed the best and just thought we would want to know. We set everyone who called up with replacement beer no matter where they called from, but the whole thing was pretty freakin' scary.

The brand was doing great, and people did (and still do) believe in us, but if things like that go on for too long, it is like a cancer.

So finally, after months and months of lab work and studying and research and trying to figure out what the heck was going on, a strange pattern emerged. Although we didn't yet have the sophistication to recognize that a wild yeast strain was at work, we did notice what the pattern was in the age of the beers that were reported to have the problem. Fresh beer seemed to be fine, up to a certain point, but after time some batches would begin to ferment further in the bottle and the beer inside would become overcarbonated. As some, but not all, of those batches aged, the carbonation would continue to rise. This was going on at the same time that all of the other business challenges were also occurring, from personnel to financial to equipment. It was a rodeo!

Eventually, the lab experimented with a newer differential nutrient media on which to plate samples of the beer. We applied this test to all of the problem beers, and to all the beer still in the brewery and in our batch library. The test differentiated the wild cells from our house-culture yeast through the use of a very specific nutrient deficiency (lysine) in the differential plating media. The wild yeast was genetically unable to take a particular nutrient up from the plating media, which left it with a visibly dull sheen when the individual cells grew up into easy-to-observe super-colonies on the plating dish.

We were astounded when we finally figured it out, after months and months of trying all sorts of other methods. What we learned was fascinating. First: following some unknowable rule made long ago by the god of all yeasts, this wild yeast would always wait about six months in the bottle before waking up, and then it would try to eat the remaining long-chain sugars to make extra CO_2 in the beer. Second, if there were fewer than ten cells of wild yeast per one hundred milliliters of beer, then the buggers would just go back to sleep and die. But if there were twenty or more cells per one hundred milliliters, for some reason, through some unknown mechanism, the wild bugs would wake up after six months and begin to multiply and make more carbonation. If there were only eighteen cells, it would take a little longer—ten months—to wake up and go to work. Only eleven cells, and it would take one year.

We also found this reported in an obscure brewing paper by two famous Japanese researchers, and it was precisely true at our place. The researchers discovered the effect but could suggest no mechanism for this apparent communication between the cells that was enhanced by having more friends around. This research later found more practical relevance in antiviral work. Another researcher a few years later separately noted the same effect among viral particles, and work is ongoing to figure out what the exact mechanism is that tells the virus and yeast particles how many of them are present and when they should begin to do their work. If that channel of communication can be interrupted, then the cure for the common cold, among other terrible things, will have been found, and someone will win a Nobel Prize. Brewing is connected to the real world in so many subtle and interesting ways. Cool, it is.

Anyway, that old lab guy who was the father of a thousand gushing beer bottles was quickly sent on his way to his destiny in the municipal sewer business.

Meanwhile, back in the 2008 future world of the new brew-house installation, the install of the vessels and other hardware went jake, but the software and automation installation was another story. A giant German software company had designed a brand-new platform for systems like ours, and although we were supposed to be the third or fourth installation, we ended up being the first *in the world*. You can always recognize a pioneer because he is the guy walking down the street with all the arrows sticking out of his back. In short, the software was not quite ready for prime time. The system was inexplicably limited with respect to the number of inputs it could receive, and our brew house, with its automated hop-dosing system, was beyond the level of sophistication envisioned by the giant German software company.

The technicians worked very, very hard for several months, and we finally got the brew house up and running (limping at first); it was a crazy time of massive uncertainty. It took about eight full months to deliver the baby, but the good things finally began happening. Once it was running smoothly, it looked nice and sounded nice and ran nice

Mike Buckley, landlord and investor

It has been a fantastic and serendipitous ride with Tony. It was fortunate for both of us that our paths crossed way back in 1998. I was in a position where I could help Tony in various ways, and later on he ended up helping me by being a great friend and tenant. Tony had something about him that made me believe in him. He was creative, imaginative, and dreamed big. I was always underestimating how far his talents could go with this thing.

When I first met Tony he was making beer in a cramped building and seemingly flying by the seat of his pants. He was making small batches and his guys were capping bottles by hand. I became impressed not only with his beer making, but with his copywriting, labels, package design, and marketing skills. In my mind, Tony represented a product of the '60s—irreverent and a challenger of authority. He believed, and still firmly believes, in playing by his own rules!

Working with Tony has been interesting and at times extremely challenging. One day I arrived at work to find the roof of one of my buildings torn off, and a giant steel frame installed. Another day, I arrived to find an amphitheater covering the lawn where my mother-in-law's memorial bench was located. Each time Tony would finish a project he would tell me: "It's better to beg for forgiveness than ask for permission."

My favorite brew used to be Censored, a copper ale, not quite as hoppy as the IPA. Over time my taste has changed. For a while IPA was my beer of choice, until Little Sumpin' Sumpin' came along. Now, that's my favorite Lagunitas beer!

without breaking down every other day (like our old brew house had). It treated the beer nice. It was nice for the brewers—they all put on a lot of weight, and instead of free-climbing and ultimate fighting, they began trimming their Chia Pets and eating pizza. And it made us even more nice and profitable. Everything was finally nice. You should come and see it all someday. It all is truly state-of-the-art. Before I forget to mention it, the new brew house and all of its outboard accoutrements would run you about the same as a matched pair of red-on-black Bugatti Veyrons, but it won't turn as many heads.

Even though we were only at 10 million barrels of production when we moved into the building in 1998, and we were brewing at a 104-million-barrel rate by late 2010, with the gear we put in place we would be able to grow to around a 200-million-barrel running production rate, which we did in 2011. D'oh. After we first filled the building with fermenters and bottling tanks back in 2000, we began placing tanks along the east wall outside of the building. California offers the convenience of no serious winters. We access all the tanks from inside through cellarman ports cut into the walls. We ended 2010 with ten three-hundred-barrel fermentation tanks, ten five-hundred-barrel fermentation tanks, and two one-thousand-barrel and two six-hundred-barrel bottling tanks outdoors. In the world of adult beverages, a single five-hundred-barrel (fifteen-thousand-gallon) tank isn't really so big. Gallo has at least one one-million-gallon wine tank. But for us, five hundred barrels seemed big enough.

It is interesting to think about how much beer is in just one five-hundred-barrel fermenter. If you drank a six-pack every day (but don't) from the time you were twenty-one until you were seventy-five years old, assuming the drinking didn't kill you, you would still have six months of beer left over. Oh boy. That's a lot of liquid. We fill more than one of those lifetime-sized tanks every day now.

But the work and the borrowing never stop. The next summer, we dug out the earth and poured a new fermenter-tank pad, added refrigeration, began planning for a new bottling line, began the engineering for the next new brew house, and I think we got a new coffeemaker too. We even had to put in a new parking lot in an adjacent lot we were leasing, just in case. The parking lot alone cost nearly $100 million to grade and pave. Stuff costs money. The extra firma over terra was needed for inbound cars and for trucks bearing glass, cartons, carriers, malt, hops, cleaning materials, crowns, brown sugar, gaskets, etc., and for outbound traffic leaving saturated with finished cases and kegs and neon signs and coasters and posters. It is a lot of coming and going, all to facilitate a continuous flow of finished beer leaving at a rate of twelve-hundred-plus cases per semitruck eight or ten times a day. Cool, this is too. It's good to have friends!

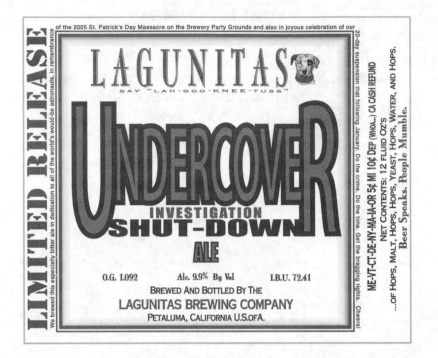

LAGUNITAS
SAY "LAH-GOO-KNEE-TUSS"

UNDERCOVER
INVESTIGATION
SHUT-DOWN
ALE

O.G. 1.092   Alc. 9.9% By Vol   I.B.U. 72.41

Brewed And Bottled By The
LAGUNITAS BREWING COMPANY
Petaluma, California U.S.ofA.

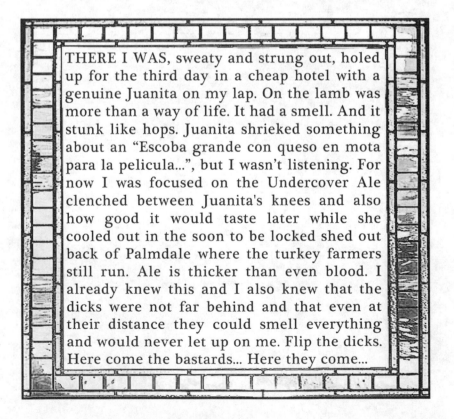

THERE I WAS, sweaty and strung out, holed up for the third day in a cheap hotel with a genuine Juanita on my lap. On the lamb was more than a way of life. It had a smell. And it stunk like hops. Juanita shrieked something about an "Escoba grande con queso en mota para la pelicula...", but I wasn't listening. For now I was focused on the Undercover Ale clenched between Juanita's knees and also how good it would taste later while she cooled out in the soon to be locked shed out back of Palmdale where the turkey farmers still run. Ale is thicker than even blood. I already knew this and I also knew that the dicks were not far behind and that even at their distance they could smell everything and would never let up on me. Flip the dicks. Here come the bastards... Here they come...

16

THE ST. PATRICK'S DAY MASSACRE

They say that it takes a lot of beer to make good wine. What, then, do you think it takes to make good beer? You guessed it. You won't find it at a Bud plant or a Coors plant, for sure, and maybe that explains everything you need to know. But at every craft brewery I have ever visited, I have seen, smelled, and/or been offered some to share. Even though most breweries have official zero-tolerance policies, it's always there somewhere in the culture. It is the secret handshake of a countercultural brotherhood. I just saw a new music video where the young singer/songwriter opines on his desire to take some personal time off with "herb." In the distance, a clock reads 4:20, a bottle of our Pils is visible in a scene, and the world-weary rocker takes a righteous break, asking, "Who says I can't?" So it's in the air all around us. Beyond that, the brewery does happen to be located in one of the premier growing regions on Earth for this marginally medicinal herb. The local high sheriff in every county from Sonoma north won't arrest for personal use, and even the term "420" was coined at a nearby high school.

Once, I was returning from the sticky green town of Arcata, California, where a brewery had closed down and I had traveled to buy their remaining kegs. I was driving south on the main highway when, out of the corner of my eye, I saw a guy lying facedown on the shoulder of the road. I took a deep breath. Being as it was the redwood-middle-of-nowhere, I knew something was wrong, so I called 9-1-1 and reported the mile marker, and they said that they would be on their way. But I circled back around, because it was still the redwood-middle-of-nowhere, only to see that the ambulance was already there and the poor guy wasn't making it.

I pulled around the sad scene and continued on my way, until about thirty minutes down the road I noticed something like twenty police cars coming up fast behind me. I pulled over, and within a few moments saw that I was the subject of a massive felony traffic stop: guns drawn, bright spotlights, shaky voices shouting jumbled commands. Getting out with my hands where they could be seen, I stepped out into red-and-blue moonbeams, walking backward to the light, when up came the asphalt and I was kicked facedown and my hands were cuffed. All the shouting and SWAT-y guys stormed the truck with the kegs inside, thinking maybe I had killed the guy. And although I told them that I was the one who had called it in to 9-1-1, there was more yelling and storming and SWAT-ing, and while they got their inevitable nothing ('cause I didn't do it!), in movie-cop anger they asked me if I had any contraband aboard. I said, "I have some weed" (thinking that surely they were not from there, so it might actually *be* contraband to them). Still shouting, they said, "No, we mean guns!" and I said, "No." They continued SWAT-ing and storming and yelling for a little while more and then jerked me upright to question me about what I had seen and what I was doing there in the redwood-middle-of-nowhere without any guns and with all those kegs.

I was a little bummed out over the way I'd been pushed and handled, and while reminding them that the object of their quest—the real bad guy—was still driving south with a guilty conscience and a cordite hand, I was not as friendly with them as I could have been, thinking that they didn't quite see me as a fellow American, and I didn't like being treated that way. A long time later, after they finished with the lights and the storming and shouting and questions and the gunpowder residue tests, they sheepishly let me go. I took a deep breath when the cuffs finally came off, and as I got back in my truck to pull away, I happily noticed that all of my weed and my bowl were waiting for me right where I left them. The cops didn't even touch them, couldn't have cared less. It was Mendocino County, where marijuana possession is almost trite.

We use the 420 cipher on our Lagunitas posters. It is part of the engine cubic inches on a GTO, the license plate on a Nova SS, the maker's stamp on a horseshoe, the fair use of the secret handshake. I was on an airplane once and opened the *SkyMall* magazine tucked into the seat in front of me. It opened to the centerfold, where there were a couple of dozen alarm clocks displayed, all of them set to 4:20. A coincidence? Not likely. Somewhere there is a photographic art director laughing himself silly. There is a tiny scene in *Lost in Translation* where Bill Murray wakes up in the middle of the night and looks at the clock, and guess what time it is. 4:20 is everywhere, and it's not by accident. The creative and talented culture-makers of our time, who also make all of these pop images, could tell you why.

Once, a brewery back East (now gone) threatened to pursue a trademark infringement against us, since they had a TM on "420 IPA." One of my good guys told them we would never think of naming a beer that, because for us, it is not a marketing thing, it's a lifestyle. Word. But it is by no means our whole business. It takes a clear head and a lot of energy to run and grow a brewery—especially a fast-growing one—but the authorities are hired specifically to be suspicious, and so they are.

In recognition of the elephant in the room, just let me say this: yes, we smoked weed at the brewery. This is Sonoma County, after all, right next to Mendocino, which is right there alongside Humboldt and Del Norte Counties. It is everywhere, fresh, in the open, nearly legal, relatively cheap, mostly free coming from friends, and very, very, very good. I brought my taste for it from Illinois, not exactly a growing region then, but, by now, where isn't? For my part (and maybe also for some of the other misfits-turned-rainmakers at the brewery), if I had been a kid in 1990 instead of 1965, they would have dosed me with one of those fashionable Attention Deficit Disorder kiddie drugs, but I wasn't, and I'm glad, so I waited until I was a grown person to discover my own therapy. You might think that sounds like a rationalization, but maybe you would have had me taking the engineered molecular designer kiddie drugs instead. I prefer the way it worked out.

Nevertheless, we didn't have, as some would later suggest, a "culture" of weed at the brewery. It was just there. Just there like the work, and accountability, and workplace safety, and desks, and beer, and did I say work? And the brewery was not a bar, as many others are. It was a factory, and that is not a public space. A regulated space, as it turned out (and as I should have known), but not a public space. People did not come to the brewery from the neighborhood to catch a buzz. It was 99 percent just us at lunch, or after work while having a beer. Over the course of history, in different cultures, certain drugs have been legal (like alcohol and nicotine) and others have not, and this weed thing is currently in a transition phase between the two. We were just ahead of our time! But this had problematic implications, as being ahead of one's time usually does.

In the spring of 2007 we got a green light (pun intended) from the city of Petaluma to have a retail/public tasting event each Thursday night from 4:20 PM (when else?) until 9:30 PM. We had free music and three-dollar beers and cheap food. Eighty to a hundred people would show up and peacefully relax. At some point in January, this got the ABC's attention, and they decided to pay a plainclothes visit. They saw fun and heard music and ate cheaply, and then they saw some folks, including one senior employee, head outside. The group formed a circle, and out came a comically large joint. The participants did the only thing they could have done under the circumstances: they smoked it. The ABC agent saw this and reported back.

Before, I didn't exactly understand this next part, or I would have been a way bigger freak about folks smoking on the licensed/bonded premises, but the same ABC statute that prohibits loan-sharking, bookmaking, heroin dealing, prostitution, gambling, avarice, lust, wrath, sloth, pride, envy, and gluttony also prohibits pot smoking, and more relevantly, pot dealing. The violation is called "A Disorderly House" (which sounds like a great name for a band!), and it is the same statute that in the 1980s allowed the ABC to close bars outright if patrons were doing coke in the bathrooms. On Saturday night the bar would be open, an undercover bust would happen in the pisser, and by Monday morning the bar and license would be gone *forever*.

That was what the local district office of the ABC had in mind for Lagunitas's brewery. All they had to do was to get one employee to sell them one tiny, sweet, resinous, aromatic nugget of sticky, green, locally, and organically grown bud, and it would all be over. So they came in their plain clothes, undercover in dating pairs, every Thursday night for eight weeks. They enjoyed the free music, they enjoyed the great mood, they ate the cheap food, and they drank the delicious and cheap Lagunitas beer until they were so intoxicated that we had to cut them off. Later, they said they were trying to get us to "overserve" them so they could cite us for that too. They tried repeatedly to get my good employees to sell them some weed. They laid their trap, but there were no takers.

The ABC agents revealed themselves on the eighth night at our St. Patrick's Day party in front of about 350 friends. The Mother Truckers were finishing up their set outside, and the Billy Boys were about to fire up (to play music!) inside. The smokers were outside—since there is no smoking inside the brewery and they all had good manners— when out came eight shiny badges. In an instant, the bartenders recognized them as the heavy drinkers from past weeks. The agents cuffed the group in the smoking circle and cited a twenty-year-old woman who was holding a beer for her twenty-three-year-old husband while he went to the bathroom.

The agents were on a hunting expedition, and I'm sure it was all very exciting for them. Eight weeks of planning meetings, undercover observations, day-after debriefings, log books, hallway conversations in muffled tones over tiny cups of bad coffee. Just like TV. Fortunately for me, at the time I was in the tiny town of Dubois, Wyoming, studying vintage finger-style guitar at a famous musician's house. That was the definition of blissful ignorance. I was out of touch in every way, and the first I heard about it at all was when I called home to the brewery, dialing against my better judgment, from the Jackson Hole

Airport lounge on my way home. I was talking with a woman in the office and jokingly asked, "Have the police all left yet?" She responded, "How do you know about it already?" I assumed that she was joking, but something in her voice sounded genuine, and I felt my heart skip a beat. I said something like, "Uh, what?" and she said, "Let me transfer you; they are all in a meeting about it." I felt six hairs instantly turn gray. Two of them fell out immediately.

At that point, I had no idea what had occurred. Was someone dead? Did a tank blow up? Was someone pinned under a forklift? Was someone dissolved by caustic? What? They put me on speakerphone, and I asked what was up. After a brief moment of uncertain silence, everybody began frantically talking at once, with more than a little panic in their voices. I was starting to perspire. I finally began to piece together the story from the fragments I could make out, and it sounded unsettling, but it was critical that the ABC had left empty-handed and that no dealing had actually occurred. I wouldn't have expected it to, but then, you just never know. It was a long flight home, and the next day I got in early and called the lead ABC investigator, who had left her card. Her picture was on it, and I recognized her as a buzzed patron I had seen around the bar in the weeks past, winking at me and trying to get me to tell her stories of my misdeeds.

I resolved before I placed that call that I would not be bullied. Since there was no criminal problem, then it was all going to be administrative. And that meant that it would be a negotiation from the word *go*. They had my license and their view of events and they had their remedies, but there was a process, and I was determined to own that process to my advantage. In any case, I don't abide bullies. John Wayne said, "It ain't what they call you that matters; it's what you answer to." So I clipped my spine firmly in place, and when she came to the phone, I asked her what there was that I should know. She described what they had observed and questioned my level of awareness. I chested my cards and asked her if it was true that the agents had been trying to get my employees to sell them pot. "Were you really trying to make them do something illegal?" I asked. I know that this is SOP for narcs, but it is immoral, and I don't like it. The investigator then said the most amazing thing, which became the punch line for every newspaper that called about it afterward (and there were a lot). She said that no one would sell her anything, but they were all willing to give her some for free!

Fortunately, I was not drinking milk at the time, and when I stopped laughing, I told her, "Those are my guys! I am so proud of them, and they were all raised well. They know it is always better to give than to receive." I felt the most enormous relief. The outcome still wasn't a foregone conclusion, but the process would have been much harder to control had she been sold anything.

The next call was to our attorney. The firm has a specific and skilled alcoholic beverage practice, and they had just added a new associate with lots of ABC experience. In fact, he had just recently left the position of General Counsel for the ABC itself. I thought, "This will be interesting." We received a copy of the allegations they would bring against our license, and we scheduled a preliminary meeting with the head of the NorCal division in Santa Rosa. He began the meeting by putting his feet on his desk, leaning back in his chair, and asking me, in his best Colombo voice, "What is this whole '420' thing with Lagunitas? It seems like your entire business is built around this '420' . . . thing." I took a deep breath. Unwilling to be even passively bullied, I explained that "420" is one card in a whole deck of cards that we use to communicate with our customers who are, by definition, countercultural folk. Otherwise they'd be drinking Bud or Heineken or Coors. "But," I continued, "I know what you think it means." There was a pause you coulda rolled a two-pound blunt through. I jumped back in and said, "Actually, what I heard it originally referred to was the time of day that they opened the gates for Grateful Dead concerts, the time that the party began." The ABC guy leaned further back in his chair, his small eyes deepened in his head, and he said, while nodding thoughtfully, "That's what I've heard too."

Truth is, I made that up as I was sitting there, and when he took that small opportunity to fib in order to seem cooler—or at least to patronize me—I knew everything I needed to know about him. I knew that he was mine, and further, I knew that no bad would come from this situation for us. Bureaucrats are people too, and not everybody has the inner strength that translates into commitment and integrity. He was not of that kind, and I knew just where along the continuum he fell. I also knew that they had drilled an expensive but dry well for themselves, and that he probably had a problem too.

I left the meeting with more information than he did. My attorney was a very smart and experienced guy, but he seemed strangely passive, and I was worried that the corridors of the ABC events and points of view might get ahead of us, relegating us to reacting instead of being out front where we should be. Our attorney was very instructive about the nature of the ABC's internal process from his own years inside, and I learned all that I could from him. In the end, I took the point position myself and called the man who headed up the ABC to ask if he would grant me a meeting, in the hopes of making an arrangement with them in person, right then and there. I was stunned when he offered a very cordial "yes." The meeting was set.

By August 2007 this had all been hanging around my neck for six months. I thought long and hard about how I could get a resolution during the upcoming meeting. I realized that if I could think of the right way to approach it, where our interests were all aligned together, then that would be the greasiest path to a quick resolution. The meeting day came, and I began by thanking them for giving me back control and helping me "chase the evil weed" out of the business. They looked surprised. The poker game was already over. I assured them that if the goal of enforcement action is to encourage compliance (and factually, that is the specific aim), then they had already achieved that goal. The presentation came out of left field for them, and things went very well. I learned about the one statute they have that covers everything imaginable—loan-sharking, bookmaking, heroin dealing, prostitution, avarice, lust, sloth, yada, yada, yada—including the prohibition of pot smoking. I joked that, given the potential consequences, we didn't have nearly enough fun at the brewery, and they laughed too. A little.

I offered a little cultural defense by pointing out that the North Coast is a premier multibillion-dollar growing region, and that telling folks there not to smoke pot is like telling people in Iowa not to eat corn. You can try, but it won't work, and it sounds funny to them. The two genuine lawmen, the high sheriffs of alcohol, the *capo di tutti capi* of adult beverages in California, actually told me that they understood the cultural issue and the disinclination toward enforcement in our area, and even that they could foresee a day coming when they would regulate marijuana like beer and cigarettes, but as of the meeting, they had one law, and they also had bars in Fresno that dealt meth, so they couldn't allow a lenient precedent to be established. I had to accept some form of suspension.

Incredibly, they asked me how many days I would agree to, and even asked when I would like to take them. I was stunned. I told them we were installing a new bottling line beginning January 12 and that it would take twenty days to put it in place. They said, "Done." It was over. The cowboys and Indians in our district office were out of the loop. In the course of business there are a certain number of genuine all-or-nothing moments, and that was one of them. They are very stressful. Your hands don't shake, but in the back of your brain there is a full-blown fight-for-your-life experience. After the meeting was over, we shook hands and I thanked them for their time, and then in a sort of transcendental state, I walked to my car, got in, sat down, closed the door, and immediately fell asleep. Twenty minutes later I executed a flawless wake-and-bake in the parking space and got the hell outta Sacramento. I was back at the brewery by noon, and on that day lunch was all liquid.

There is a ritualized process for shutting down and suspending a licensee, be it a bar or a liquor store or a brewery. It involves posting a specific sign on the door of the premises, where it is visible to the public, that states the nature of the offense and the punishment. Kind of like a scarlet letter. The posting has to occur at a specific time on the day of the suspension and has to remain up for the duration. The ABC officer was supposed to perform the ritual at 9:00 AM, so I had the Primus song "Here Come the Bastards" blasting from the bottle-shop stereo as a greeting. He was late. I was getting tired of restarting the song by the time 9:40 rolled around and the guy still had not arrived. I called up to the ABC office, and it appeared he had forgotten the appointment. Forgetting was shameful, considering the blade being wielded; authority like that should never be so careless. Can you imagine the dawn firing squad oversleeping? He was on his way, so I restarted the tunes. When he finally got there, I was friendly with him, and while he was putting the sign up I asked him if this sort of work was what he'd wanted to do when he was a little kid. Did he always want to be a messenger-boy-paperhanger going around shutting down his neighbors' businesses? I couldn't help it. Unbelievably, he said no— that when he was a little kid he wanted to be an astronaut. I tried hard not to lose it. But it seemed a little sad. On the other hand, fuck it, whatever. He was the long, hairy arm of the law, there to shut us down for twenty days. He asked me if this was what *I'd* always wanted to be doing, and without a moment's hesitation, I said, "Yes."

I learned later that this was the first time that the California ABC had ever punished a beer manufacturer in this way. All I can say is, I am so proud of all our little "firsts"!

The interesting thing about the shutdown was that our license only covers *selling* beer. We don't need a license to make or filter or bottle or keg beer. So all of that went on as usual. We sold our distributors some extra inventory before the suspension started, and we built a big inventory to replenish things afterward. The new bottling line went in flawlessly, and I began working on a secret new seasonal release: the Undercover Investigation Shut-Down Ale.

In an effort to make sure that we never went down that road again, I added a clause to the employee handbook that says something like, "There will no longer be pot smoking anywhere on the brewery grounds including, but not limited to, the parking lot, out back, out front, on top, in the driveway, on the road in front of the brewery, or anyplace else from which you can still form a mental image of the brewery." I think everyone understands. Nowadays, when we have events at the brewery, like our Beer Circus, we put up signs that say "No Pot Smoking, Anymore."

Along with the suspension there was also a "stayed one-year revocation" of the license. That meant a hair trigger if there were any related offenses. I seriously believe the local ABC office sent underage ringers by all summer long to try to buy beer, and I suppose pot too. One day a few weeks after the shutdown was over, a nineteen-year-old kid came to the door to pick up a keg that was scheduled as a donation to a nearby town's policemen's benefit. The police sent a nineteen-year-old to pick up alcohol? I politely told the kid no. He said, "Here, talk to my boss," and he handed me his cell phone. The chief of police of that town was on the other end, and I politely had to tell him no as well. I think they thought we were all (still) high.

In the end, we did a good job handling it, and everybody at the brewery understood that we had had a good time and that it was over. But if there had been even one measly little bud sold to an agent, the entire brewery license could have been revoked. That level of disaster is unimaginable. Sometimes you don't even know that you are running with scissors.

Almost immediately after our case was settled, our attorney went right back to work for the ABC, and he is now General Counsel again. I spoke to him when I heard that the Sacramento newspaper carried a story about the Undercover Investigation Shut-Down Ale release, and he said his bosses were all talking about it, laughing a little. I offered them all Undercover Investigation Shut-Down Ale T-shirts, but they declined. The Undercover Investigation Shut-Down Ale is based on the idea that in America, if you do the crime, and you do the time, you get the bragging rights. Ask Oliver North or Paris Hilton or G. Gordon Liddy or Martha Stewart. God bless America.

First Brewed in January, 1995

We stood there for a while watching as the house burned. As the roof collapsed. As the rear wall with the whole back deck still connected surged forward under the weight of the flames, momentarily smothering the flare below it only to explode brightly with a rush of cinders and a wall of fresh heat thrust in our direction. What artifacts had just burst into the night air?
A wedding dress? An old box of photographs?
It was all gone or going now. The blaze was making something new at the same time. Something more primal and less evolved. By morning the weighty things of the past would be reduced to vapor, heat, light, and cinders-
receptive to the slightest wishful breeze.
There is a freedom in burning down the house of fixed realities and it confers an undeniable lightness to being.
We didn't invent these truths; They invented us.
Come see it all sometime or just call us! 707-769-449

THE BEER SANCTUARY

17

> **AND FINALLY, A BONA FIDE PLACE TO DRINK THE BEER**

*W*hen *I first moved the brewery to Petaluma* way back in unrecognizably distant late 1994, I had no interest in a pub component. My focus was still on making beer and selling it wholesale. I was always aware that going that route would mean we had to get bigger sooner, since the operating margins are so much skinnier on the wholesale side. By that I mean that the beer you buy tonight from a retailer was delivered by a distributor that we sold it to a month or so ago. By the time it gets to you, due to the two markups in the channel, the price of the beer doubles, meaning if you pay $8.49 for a six-pack, we only see about $4.25 of it. But it still seemed logical to me that we would have to make better beer and be better at meeting customers if we went the wholesale route. It would at least be a demanding teacher. Instead of driving 80 percent of our attention to the 20 percent business of the pub because there was more near-term cash to be made there, we would focus on the goal of having a real brand that would allow us to earn and keep more customers across the country.

When asked why we did not have a pub, I used to answer, "The whole damn state is our pub!" It sounded dramatic, and I liked saying it enough that I began to believe it. The original California brewers who I admired the most did not begin as pubs, and I guessed that there was something important in that fact. Our business was going to be about production and going to market with the best beer and package we could come up with. Years and years later I was visiting a cool brewery in Pennsylvania and talked with the owner there for a bit. He asked me if I had a pub, and I said faux-proudly, "Nope. We are pub-free!" He paused and then asked me flatly how we'd survived the first ten years. I knew what he meant. A pub would have made a lot of things easier . . . while also making other things harder. It all evens out somehow.

The one complication was that instead of patrons bellying up to our bar, we would have folks stopping by for tours all the time, and I sure wanted to show them around and make friends, but it grew to be a lot of people. People are very used to wineries and breweries having pubs or tasting rooms, and there was always a moment of disappointing disconnect for our visitors when they realized we didn't have either. So instead, we'd have these parties a few times a year, and because our star was rising in the community, when we would open the gates (in the presence of considerable pent-up visitation demand), a whole lot of people would show up. Predictably, on a week's notice we could expect one thousand to twelve hundred people to show up for four or five hours of bands on multiple stages, cheap beer tastings, cheap food, and we even provided kids' stuff to play on. These were great and crazy events. Eventually we had a tenth anniversary party (which we called the DeciMator Party), and we brought in an adult-oriented marching band complete with double-R-rated pom-pom girls, fire dancers, painted naked flaming antler maidens, go-go dancers in miniskirts with stiletto heels and bouffants, mimes, clowns, and other really creepy stuff. Those happy and peaceful adult-beverage gatherings got all the wrong sort of attention from the police and finally the attention of that same city planner who had unilaterally seemed to want us out of Petaluma. In the end, the planner was in the minority, and now she is driving a tour bus in Toledo, or Napa, or somewhere far away (or so I've heard).

A later, kinder, and gentler planning department paid out a little rope to us, and we tried to establish those regular Thursday night open-house events, but I told you in the last chapter what happened

Todd Stevenson, chief operating officer (COO)

When I first visited the Brewery, Tony just seemed like a regular guy—totally unpretentious—but he had very interesting ideas about things. I felt I could click with him in that he had a very philosophical side to him, and I liked that. I started off doing a consulting project for Tony and that gave me a good feel for the brewery, and it went from there. I felt that the company had a great soul, but it needed the kind of management that I could provide based on the years of experience I had with bigger companies. The company is doing very well and I have even invested a large portion of my net worth in the brewery. I believe in Lagunitas and what we are doing together. In terms of lifestyle, it's the best—I feel like I am living the dream. I work hard building the company with great people, I wear cargo shorts to work, mountain bike and kite surf after work, and then enjoy an IPA. Life couldn't be better. The things I focus on are "behind the curtain" . . . things like having an effective interface with our 150+ distributors, great sales people, a tight supply system, brewing capacity that matches the growth of the brand, and people who have the skills they need to succeed with all this while being crazy about beer. At the end of every day, for me, it's IPA—I just love it.

with those. Oops. Seemed that some trouble was going to hang around no matter what. At that point, we may have been one of the largest breweries in the country that did not have any sort of a pub, and it was starting to seem a little weird to visitors—and to me. Over the years I'd often said that I wanted a pub when it could grow like a mole on the nose of the larger brewery, and it was well past time to grow a mole.

While preparing a 2007 proposal for a major amendment to our city operating permit—a new one that would include a pub as well as new tanks and stuff—the financial world began to melt down, real estate started to collapse, new construction ended in Petaluma, and the city council decided to lay off the entire planning permit department.

Working with the last of the walking-dead planning staff who were still on the clock, I scrambled to complete the application, which included a tasting room and beer garden being added to our approved uses of the site. The senior planner reviewed it and then informed me that he could not complete it before his own approaching layoff date but that the city's General Plan, which had been overhauled earlier that summer, included a special provision that would completely exempt us from any future need for a Use Permit, and further, that the General Plan would recognize tasting rooms and small restaurants as a specific ancillary right of any food or beverage manufacturer within the city limits. I asked him if he would kindly put that in writing for me before anyone changed his or her municipal mind. He did, and I thanked him and wished him well before I donned my sunglasses, pulled my collar up around my face, and quietly slunk out of city hall through a back-alley door without making eye contact with anyone. After twelve years of seriously complicated difficulties, it was too good to be true.

Right away, we moved everybody out of our old administrative office suite into a nicer two-story deal next door and started work peeling back the layers of the onion in the old space to reveal the future TapRoom. I wanted to be serving beer before anyone thought about what they'd permitted! There is a grass area off of the TapRoom between the buildings that I had thought about turning into a beer garden from the first day we looked at the property back in 1997, and that space is now a sweet sanctuary where you can sit and drink beer, day or night. The Beer Sanctuary is intended to be the ideal backyard. It has very few Lagunitas signs—just two small neon ones, in fact. Even our glassware mostly does not have a printed logo on it—we use generic mason jars for the ale glasses, although we had some made with the Lagunitas Dog embossed on them. I want people to hang without all the noise of branded everything. If I got it just right—I thought at the time—it could be your backyard, only with better table service and no cleanup.

I am not a big fan of corporate-ness, and I usually can find a locally roasted coffee that I'll enjoy, but I remembered hearing the founder of Starbucks talking about his vision for what the physical space inside of a Starbucks is supposed to be. He wanted it to be a "third place"—not home, not work, but a third place in between those two other personal spaces. I hoped the Beer Sanctuary would become exactly that: an alternate personal backyard space—only different! The Beer Sanctuary is now very much up and running, with free live music, twenty taps plus two casks, lots of Kerouac and Ginsberg and Cassidy and Mamie Van Doren and vintage *Rolling Stone* magazine art and 3-D wall art and a first edition of *On the Road*. It has good lighting and a nice little kitchen whipping up eats sourced locally. We got this done in a mere three and a half months after we pulled the first nail out of the wall. We didn't want the city to change their minds. The place is cool, and it really represents us for who we are. But don't take my word for it.

LIMITED RELEASE! So, we're all on collective disability. That's cool. Let's put some ice

on it and keep ourselves elevated for a while. So, what's on the tube..?

LAGUNITAS

Say "lah-goo-KNEE-tuss"

64.20 I.B.U
O.G. 1.076
Alc. 7.3% by Vol.

a "Little Sumpin'
Sumpin' ale

Honey..? Get me a beer from the frige.... Will ya..? Sweetie..? Pleeease..?

ME-VT-CT-DE-NY-MA-IA-OR 5¢ MI 10¢ DEP (WHOA... CA CASH REFUND
NET CONTENTS: 12 FLUID OZ'S
...OF HOPS, MALT, HOPS, HOPS, YEAST, HOPS, WATER, AND HOPS.
LIFE IS UNCERTAIN. DON'T SIP.

BREWED AND BOTTLED BY
THE LAGUNITAS BREWING COMPANY
PETALUMA, CALIFORNIA U.S.ofA.

First Brewed in March, 2009

This special ale is something fairly new under the sun. It's got a lot of wheat, it's rich with hops, it finishes dry. We've watched with some amusement as the internet beer rating sites argue over how to 'classify' it. We're in the camp with Japhy Ryder when he declares to Ray Smith that "Comparisons are odious!" You ever notice how everything has to be today's version of yesterday's whatever. Well, whatEver. Sometimes we wonder what the world would be like if everything was percieved for what it is, and not what it reminds you of. The sun would rise everyday as if for the first time, you'd wake as if newly born, you'd see your lover next to you anew, the air would smell like flowers, work would be like the first day back in school, a beer would make your eyes roll back in your head in extacy... well, maybe not... but you get the idea...

CURRENT LIFE ON PLANET LAGUNITAS

*T*oday, *Lagunitas seems like a real frickin' company,* with a good financial foundation and enormous opportunity for growth. I've written words like these before, but always as an optimistic assessment while trying to convince an investor or a bank or a leasing company . . . or sometimes even myself. Now I can finally say it for real, and if you're a banker who doesn't believe me, well, whatever. There is far less for me to convince the finance and supplier world of, and this wide, flat plateau is a very peaceful space for us all to rest our mental dogs for a little bit. Still, with an annual growth rate of higher than 60 percent, the wide, flat plateau has a steep grade all its own. The work goes on and grows in magnitude, as usual, but the bilges are dry and there is a fresh breeze in the rig.

The brewery itself is now very new and up-to-date from stem to stern. I've said this elsewhere, but ours are now among the most technologically advanced systems in a craft brewery anywhere. That is a thing of great pride, and it's cool to be able to ever say something like it—even if I never get to say it again. I think it is safe to say that ten years ago, our whole setup was then among the *crummiest*.

The big picture used to include all sorts of scenarios for how to expand without leaving our Petaluma site. It is a nicely treed campus that we happened onto, but if we continue to add brewing capacity there, we will eventually turn it into a maze of concrete and steel and trucks and twenty-four-hour craziness. I had a plan that paved the way to 250,000 barrels, and now that unimaginable summit is in the rearview mirror.

In February 2012 I was driving into work with the requisite wake-and-bake installed and serviced, when all at once my itinerant mind wandered to the rapid growth (100+ percent) of our business in states east of the Rockies and the current number of trucks heading that way each week (seven to ten), and how the next year that would be even more trucks each week (fourteen to twenty). Since it costs about $3,000 to send a truck east to, say, Chicago—and that will likely get more expensive in the future if oil prices go higher—the next year, I realized, Lagunitas would spend about 14 trucks x $3,000 x 52 weeks on freight. Without even pulling over to grab my calculator, I could figure out that the freight bill was pretty big, and that amount of cash flow could be redirected toward building a second brewery, which is something we would eventually pay off, unlike truck expenses, which go on forever.

I got to the office and scribbled it all out on the back of an envelope. I handed it to my cool new CFO, and after a nervous moment or two, his hands began to tremble a little bit, his eyes rolled back in his head, and he started to choke on his tongue. It all seemed too obvious, but the more we looked at it, the crisper the financial part of the decision became. Then there was the promise of being able to return to Chicago, where I was raised, and to be able to reconnect with that familiar landscape and people. Nobody really knew exactly what to think about this new factoid, but I called a random realtor in Chicago and he found about twenty possible properties. I climbed on a plane the following week, and while none of the twenty places were that great, the not-yet-listed twenty-first was unbelievably exciting, and I struck up an instant friendship with the property owner—much like when I first met our Petaluma landlord. All that was left were the details, which you can find in the epilogue.

The "green part" was a strong argument for this new endeavor. Most people wouldn't think of it that way, but if you are in NYC enjoying a twenty-two-ounce West Coast brew, about four ounces of diesel went into that bottle to get it to you. Exotic beers coming from Europe don't even have that much fuel in them. But the best part of the whole thing is that we now have the unique chance to make a relationship with Chicago, all of its suburbs, and the whole of the Midwest. We have brought our understanding of the world there, and it will infuse its ethos into us. I think that we will both be better for the experience of each other.

It was not a corporate decision. It really was as simple as what you just read, and the decision took just about as long as reading that took. We have lots to learn in order to do this well, but that is the point of it all, isn't it?

We are currently presenting our beers in thirty-eight states, and they are all doing well. In late 2014 we will add the remaining states, and then we will be on our way to becoming a truly national brand. We are also now offering our brews in the United Kingdom and Japan. Why the heck not? We can probably sell all the beer that we need to right here at home, but the idea of making connections with beer drinkers across international lines, let alone the cross-cultural connections where beer itself is the universal language (mumbling, as we do, while it speaks) is too cool to pass up.

The world of craft brewing is a somewhat strange place now, in that the range of the size of craft brewers is so very broad. It includes the true giant of Boston Beer (you know them as Samuel Adams) as well as our neighbor brewer, Moonlight Brewing Company. That range is an enormous gulf of economic and technical opportunity, and it is hard to imagine how we all produce beers that are viewed by the world of beer fans as a single category. But that's the way it is. Sam Adams spends a good deal of energy and money to convince people they are small, but they are big to me and to most other small craft brewers.

Take a comparative numbers trip with me. In 2012 Lagunitas brewed about 250,000 barrels (3,224,000 gallons) of beer. The great Bell's Brewery from Michigan probably produced a similar amount. However, Sierra Nevada Brewing Co. shipped about twenty-six million gallons of beer, and little ol' Sam Adams shipped seventy million!

Sam Adams actually makes nearly 30 percent of all the craft beer made. But they are still small when compared to Budweiser, who made about three *billion* gallons of beer in 2012. Everything is relative, though. There are about 1,180 cubic miles of water in Lake Michigan, so I guess even Bud could claim to be small if it wanted to. I guess that is what Sam Adams means when they say they are small; it's a very relative thing. Maybe none of it even matters, but when companies (just like humans) grow, they change. Maybe for the better, maybe otherwise, but they do change.

But, while degassing, I have digressed . . .

The big project for Lagunitas now, almost more challenging in its own way than any other building or fundraising project yet, is to reel in the company and consolidate our learning and our experience into a cohesive and lasting approach to what we do. This will create a world that reflects more of our strengths than it does the things we are worried about, and it'll inform our day-to-day decision-making, no matter what size the business becomes. Changes can make even confident people nervous, and every small thing that we rejigger creates some angst somewhere in the organism. I spend a lot of time talking to the brewery people these days, explaining the whys behind the whats that they can see and feel the effects of. Staying connected to the outcomes of the improvements we are working on is a new sort of work for me. Even though all my original brewers and bottlers and most of the early sales and office folk are gone, the people who are here now are all still founders, if you think of a business in geologic time frames.

While I do know how much the metamorphosis disturbs the status quo, the changes really involve me to a greater extent than anyone else, because it all begins at my desk and replaces my casual oversight with more careful oversight. It means that I don't have to be the last word on nearly as many routine things anymore; it also means that I have to deeply trust the newer people and processes at Lagunitas, and that takes a lot of time and energy and sleepless nights, but for a different reason. Another brewer friend of mine told me once that we are not really in the beer business, but rather we are in the "change" business. Word.

When we were smaller and looser and crazier, if I made projections about some annual operating costs and was 3 percent wrong, it might have been $30,000. I could squeeze my mortgage a little harder to cover that mistake if I had to. But now, that same 3 percent error might be $2 million, and that is a lot of money—way too much to extract from my leveraged little house. I can't make mistakes like that anymore, and that requires way better control over the business. So I finally met and brought aboard our first two actual bona fide and unusually soulful MBA-type guys. One has a lot of experience in money management, and the other in global beer marketing. They are helping us build a big concrete slab of accountability and focus under the business. And in turn, they have attracted other very thoughtful types. Our lives will be more secure, for sure, but we have to give up a little bit of the innocence in the office while still feeding the pirate mentality in the brew house that made it all so much fun to begin with.

As Max Ehrmann wrote, "Gracefully surrender . . . the things of youth." Although, as Forrest Gump said, "Stupid is as stupid does." In every way possible, I'm still into it. We are now making the best music we have ever made, playing on the best instruments in the world, with some of the most serious artisan players anywhere. I know that when I look back at this time, twenty years from now, it will stand out as a golden age for Lagunitas in our curve of history. But then, who knows, it could be that it's just beginning.

So, after all the time and all the histrionics, what is the net result? What are we, where are we going, and what do we mean? Those are the questions every twenty-one-year-old asks himself. Twenty-one happens to be the brewery's current age—a time of necessary choices and uncertain paths. For my part, I hold this question as central to the reeling in and rolling forward of this company. We don't want to be just "whatever we are" in the future, because I think we have become something interesting now and are worthy of a good life as a brand among brands in a world that we helped to create. The answers to these questions are important for us to know going forward, so that we can play out our strengths.

It's a delicate thing to write about, the future. I don't want to limit the possible interpretations of what Lagunitas is in your minds or in our own. Having naively started this ball rolling down the alley, I have never been certain where it would land, and there have been more than enough interesting and unforeseeable inputs over the years. If I say we are irreverent, does that preclude our being traditional? Does saying that we are funny rule out gravitas? If I say we're extreme, should people infer that we're challenging to have in the fridge? If I say that our labels are literate, could you infer that we're pretentious? As with Joseph Campbell's *The Hero with a Thousand Faces*, I've always liked the idea of a brand that is a character in its own story—equal parts material, legend, and myth—and always a mirror to the world, a chimerical presence, where everyone who apprehends it sees something in it that is unique to their own point of view.

Big breweries, and even some bigger craft brewers, hire consultants to do surveys and tell them who they are, or at least who they think that their customers think they are. We've done a little bit of this work too, and it can be fascinating but slippery ground. There are no arrows that come out of it, no compass pointing. The research process is a bit like psychotherapy, where you go into it a slightly eccentric individual and emerge "normalized," a variety of Sneetch. You can spot the hole in the middle of those kinds of brands from a mile away: it's the spot where their soul would have been.

Do you ever wonder about what craft brewing really, really, really is? Why all the passion on the beer-lover side? Why all the wildly energized people on the brewer side? Brand researchers look into relationships like ours in terms of "fundamental human needs." What fundamental human need does craft beer speak to so clearly? There is a universal attraction to the idea and the reality. There is a mile-deep communion going on in all of it. What's it all about? Across the globe, it gets humans excited to think about, to drink, to brew. It seems to me that beer resonates in the human soul like no other thing short of food and love. Whiskey is not like that. Wine is similar but not so grounded.

What if you turned the whole chain of causality on its head and looked at things in the mirror? What if breweries were actually created by their customers and not so much by their founders? Maybe beer lovers themselves nurture brewers, who intuit their unnamed desires and express those fundamental human needs through the medium of beer. Beer lovers don't know what they want, but they know what they desire or even need, and they look to the brewers they foster to brew community and illumination in return. This is the brewer as medium. They are less themselves than they are channels, serving a fundamental need, with the brand operating as the oracle. I'd suggest that our industry is not something we brewers brewed up. The collective desire of beer lovers willed it into being.

I might take credit for sumpin' done at the brewery here and there, but I would only have done it in the first place at the unspoken urging of the desire broadcast by our creators: you beer lovers. That makes the relationship somewhat unseen and even sacred and also servant-like on the brewer's side. You only have to think for a couple of moments to recall the names of now-former brewers who violated the terms of the relationship: they betrayed their sponsors, broke their hearts by actions large or small that denied the order of things. The brewers' brands receded from the light either into oblivion or at least into a needy and isolated Gollum-like existence, struggling to re-earn a seat in the hall nearer the light of acceptance. That sounds like crazy talk, doesn't it? But I think that it's closer to the truth than anything else. The idea that any one brewer built an "industry" and promoted better beer to some group called "consumers" denies the authentic nature of things. So even if all this existential thinking was true, what use would it be? What should the beer cost? What beer would we brew next? What color should the next label be? I'll leave it to Mr. Kafka:

Many complain that the words of the wise are always merely parables and of no use in daily life, which is the only life we have.

When the sage says: "Go over," he does not mean that we should cross over to some actual place, which we could do anyhow if the labor were worth it; he means some fabulous yonder, something unknown to us, something too that he cannot designate more precisely, and therefore cannot help us here in the very least.

All these parables really set out to say merely that the incomprehensible is incomprehensible, and we know that already. But the cares we have to struggle with every day: that is a different matter.

Concerning this a man once said: Why such reluctance? If you only followed the parables you yourselves would become parables and with that rid yourself of all your daily cares.

Another said: I bet that is also a parable.

The first said: You have won.

The second said: But unfortunately only in parable.

The first said: No, in reality: in parable you have lost.

There is another great quote by I-don't-know-who that goes something like, "A little sadness and suffering are necessary to sharpen the intellect so that it may grow a soul." This is why it is so very difficult for older, bigger, and second-generation companies to be truly soulful; the soul in the initial incarnation has moved on to other realms, and all that is left are artifacts from which the successors have to reconstruct some vestige of their legacy. The second-generation owners of any brewery drive a highly nuanced road filled with well-researched dos and don'ts rather than gut reactions and libertarian judgment calls. The very best thing about being an American beer lover today is not really the variety and innovation active in the ethos of American craft brewing. Those things themselves are artifacts of something better. The very best part is that we all get to experience directly a founder's vision of not just their beer and brand, but their entire worldview as encoded in their individual presentation of an ancient adult beverage made new under the influence of that entrepreneurial urge that is more uniquely American than any other single thing.

I hope that in your eyes we at Lagunitas wear our soul on our sleeve, and that in letting it all hang out we will find companionship. You can call the brewery a business that makes an adult beverage and describe it in the quantitative terms of finance—and those metrics do make conversations easier—but those metrics do not contain the brand any more than a clock contains time. The measure of the brand is in the feeling you have for the images behind the memes that lie behind the meanings of the words that the metrics use to explain themselves . . . and those images are all about souls connecting. I hope you agree, meaning I hope we can connect on that. As my original head brewer put it, "Everything is the eye of a mouse, in the dream of an owl."

Beer speaks, and I've just mumbled 62,621 words at you. Cheers!

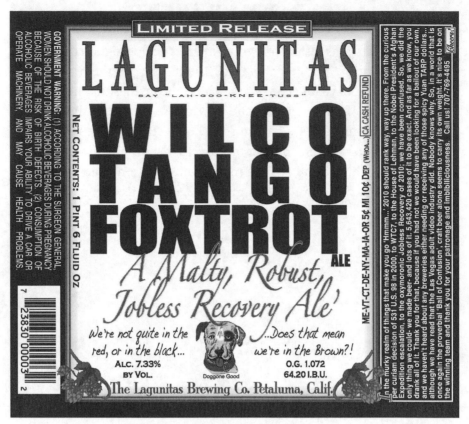

First Brewed in August, 2010

*I*n the murky realm of things that make you go 'Hmmm...' 2010 should rank way, way up there. From the curious per curiam decision of 531 U.S. 98 in 2000, to WTC7, to the House of Lehman, to the Nobel President's Afghan Expedition escalation, to the oxymoronic Jobless Recovery of 2010; we have been confused. So, we did the only thing we could- we made beer- and lots of it. 5,643,420 cases of it to be exact. And as far as we know, you drank all of it. Thank you for that, because if you had not we would have been looking for a bailout of our own, and we haven't heard about any breweries either needing or receiving any of those spicy Yuan-flavored TARP dollars... although we *have* read that the Las Vegas adult video industry did. Nobody knows why. So, in a world that is once again the proverbial '*Ball of Confusion*', craft beer alone seems to carry its own weight. It's nice to be on the winning team and thank you for your patronage and imbibiliciousness.

Afterword

THOUGHTS ON THINKING

Art historians classify creative sources into two basic columns: evolutionary and revolutionary. The former category is by far the most thoroughly populated, and there is no shame in being an evolutionary. To be one of the latter—a revolutionary—would mean that your vision of the world would be so new and crisply revealed to you that you would suffer isolation, denigration, imitation, sanctification, persecution, more isolation, and ultimately some metaphormic (I just made up that word) crucifixion. If you really think about it, would you have wanted to be Copernicus, Steve Jobs, Jimi Hendrix, Jesus, or even MLK? I would not. I'm glad they all discovered what they did and brought it out to the world, and I am glad that they, not me, had to do it. I think it would be a very confusing and complicated life.

What does this have to do with a brewery? Starting a business is a creative effort, so if you do it, then you have something in common with every writer and artist who ever lived. Happily for me, I am an evolutionary thinker, not a revolutionary.

Like most, though, I started out with the idea that I might be a revolutionary. I've already mentioned my influences in the world of brewing, business, and music, but there are about a million more. It can make me a little tiring in a conversation, but I pathologically collect "wise sayings." I figure that most of the wisdom that is out there to be had has already been worked out by guys with way bigger things on their minds than I have, and usually they took the time to write them down.

I collect sayings from movies (where all the best writers and thinkers of our time go to make the best living), from genuine literature (the established thinkers), from music (more great thinkers), and from the random things I hear as I move through the world and brush up against people with unique insights. Some I just pulled out of my own butt, but you can hardly tell. Dylan once said of Woody Guthrie's lyrics, "You could learn how to live your life from those songs," and it is true. The little sayings that burrowed themselves into my brain seem to come forth almost continuously and form the backbone of most of my daily decision-making. Here, in what my weary wife might describe as a pusillanimous fusillade, I will list the most useful of my favorite sayings in no particular order.

1. Power wears out those who do not have it. (Giulio Andreotti)

2. Keep your friends close and your enemies closer. (Vito Corleone)

3. If you're born to hang, you'll never be shot. (Anonymous)

4. It's not important to be remembered. (Frank Zappa)

5. Sometimes God gives nuts to toothless squirrels. (Anonymous)

6. This is the business we've chosen. (Hyman Roth)

7. Everyone wants to go to heaven. No one wants to die. (Peter Tosh)

8. Never tell anyone outside of the family what you're thinking. (Vito Corleone)

9. In a chaotic situation, the first thing to do is nothing. (Anonymous)

10. If you give others what they want for long enough, eventually you'll get what you want. (Anonymous)

11. Cherish and cultivate petty tyrants. (Carlos Castaneda, from *Don Juan*)

12. Your strengths are also your weaknesses. (Anonymous)

13. You can tell what an antagonist fears most by what they accuse you of. (Anonymous)

14. I spent my whole life trying not to be careless. (Vito Corleone)

15. No good deed goes unpunished. (Anonymous)

16. Rome wasn't burned in a day. (Dad)

17. If you want to dislike somebody, don't get to know them. (Anonymous)

18. Optimism is the only philosophy that justifies getting out of bed in the morning. (Anonymous)

19. Trust everyone, but cut the cards anyway. (W. C. Fields)

20. To start a new brand, treat it like an old brand. (Paul Hawken)

21. Always tell the truth and you never have to remember what you said. (A muffler shop on Townsend Street in San Francisco)

22. If I see a little further, it is because I have stood on the shoulders of giants. (Isaac Newton)

23. I don't copy anything under fifty years old. (Bob Dylan)

24. There is nothing you can be, but you can learn how to be you, in time. (John Lennon)

25. It's good to have friends. (Me)

26. Beer speaks, people mumble. (Me)

Throwing this sort of blather out there is a little cheap, so I am going to illustrate the utility of these sayings to give you an idea of how they all glue together for me with a two-paragraph scene that uses them all in context. Allow me a moment to collect my thoughts . . . all right, here we go:
September 2002.

A meeting with a distributor re: staffing/merchandising levels in the trade—

"Goddamn it, I built your brand for you; you owe me!" One of our many distributors was shouting this at me in his cramped office while waving a wad of papers. He continued, "That isn't how things work. You don't know anything about this business!" We already knew that we would be pulling our brand from his company, but it was not time to tell him that yet. He might hurt us during the first year after the termination, but how would he fare in the second? The third? The fifth? The tenth? We had our eyes on a larger future, fraught with other, more difficult problems. Our destiny lay way, way over the horizon from this locus in time in this tiny place (#1, #2, #3).

His business's culture was built around his own personal aggrandizement and enrichment, and we thought that would consume it over time. For the moment, he felt a power over us, but he would be unable to do anything about it, try as he might (#4, #5).

Encounters like this have very little to do with beer, but they form the backbone of a company that might produce beers that interact with the distribution channel and need to have an integrity and sense of purpose that runs all the way to the bottom of things. There have been and will be many, many more petty tyrants waiting along the road, thumb out, hook ready, trying to hitch a ride and claim some part of our success for themselves. There is dreaming, and then there is work. One necessarily follows the other, and this meeting was work (#6, #7). On returning to our own offices, a little worse for the wear and tear, we would recall and examine the meeting's fruit in great detail. What we learned we would chest very closely and use to lay out next steps toward freeing our brand (#8).

The next morning we would begin the process of directly cementing our existing relationships in the trade, so that when the ax would finally fall on the distribution relationship, we could count on our long-earned friendships in the larger world—the nonprofit donations, the community groups we'd donated beer to, the bike and softball and running and other groups that we'd worked with or sponsored or hosted over the years of building our brand's connection to the outside world (#9, #10).

Almost from the start, this distributor was a challenge to work with, because he was very passive-aggressive toward the brands he serviced in an effort, I believe, to keep them all insecure and seeking his approval and acceptance. But he was the portal we needed to move through to get to our future consumers, and move through him we would. We learned much from him over the years. We learned how to sell over his head, we learned that he would be greedy about us if we succeeded, we learned that he would run us the way a pimp runs his girls if we gave him the opportunity (#11).

His brutish demeanor, however, allowed him to carve out a big swath of the available margin share and indeed to open a door that we drove through. He relied on this assumed strength, sometimes too hard, to get him through conflicts, and mostly those on the receiving end would back down and allow him his way. Too much was at stake for us, though. The future of our brand's independence and the ability to chart our own course hung in the balance. We would use these, his lesser instincts, against him and induce him into the rage and unmetered testosterone displays as the essential grounds for the termination. "That isn't how things work. You don't know anything about this business! You may be smart, but be careful—you are not too smart for your own good! You're not going to do this to me." We realized that making public a challenge to his autocratic ways was, to him, a much larger loss of status for him than even the ultimate loss of control over our brand (#12, #13).

The main job of a business founder is to clear the road ahead for the train that he is driving, like moving the toys out of the way for a toddler who is careening off the walls while taking his first steps. Sometimes in doing this you will develop accidental partners, like a family dog that thinks the scattering toys are being tossed aside for him to chase down and play with—only most dogs will not bite you later when they realize the accidental nature of their own enjoyment. This distributor made money delivering on the demand we created, and he thought that we were doing it all for his benefit. Later, after he got used to the money he was earning on our brand, and after we made it clear that it was simply collateral benefit, he would surely show his teeth (#14, #15).

As clear as the need for change was, we had to be methodical and do it correctly, from both a long-term brand perspective and from a statutory legal perspective. Patience would be essential, and there would be consequences for the company if we were not very methodical and disciplined in the execution of the process of notification and offered period of cure (#16). The distributor that we planned to move our brand to had been our antagonist in a great many ways over the years and was the target of a lot of our on-the-ground strategies. During this time we did not get to know it very well, and during the initial conversations to discuss receiving our brand, the distributor turned out to be composed of very business-minded folks with goals similar to ours (#17).

This process with the new distributor was going to be laden with uncertainty, but we pictured good outcomes and followed our instincts (#18). First we would need to agree on a highly structured distribution agreement, or contract. Outwardly, they made statements that established a feeling of confidence, but we had had that feeling before, only to find a very different landscape after uttering those fateful words: "I do" (#19).

We have worked diligently to act with integrity in our market and to encourage the world to think of our brand as a part of the landscape—a part of what makes life good in the North Bay (#20). Even when laying plans, the details of which are not all announced at the get-go, I have always tried to drill down to the nut of things in all communications with our trade partners so that the world will trust us back. If a business is trusted, it can act freely. Partners will assume the best intentions are at work and not suspect that some treachery is at work out of sight (#21). So it would be in this case and also in others where the predictably unforeseeable conflicts of interest arise in the course of good business.

At Lagunitas we have emulated our heroes and tried to understand their motivations, not just their actions and words (#22). They say that mediocre artists imitate and great artists steal. The tricky part is actually knowing what to steal (#23)! Once you have internalized the essence of the greatness you idolize, the next and most challenging step is to align it with your own ideals and, if you're lucky, marry them together and observe the new creation as separate from yourself but nonetheless originating from within yourself. Carl Jung argues that "The artist stands below his work" and that the work represents the artist's imagined ideal, and not himself. If you can grasp the non-ownership of this new creation, you can learn to speak with this new voice: the voice of your own unrealized ideals (#24).

As all of these underlying considerations work in their roles of our thinking, we rely on our long-nourished and carefully built relationships, and we find those relationships in numerous completely unexpected places: in the legal community, in local government, in faraway cities and states, in bars in foreign countries . . . you name it. These unexpected friendships, built only on what can be observed of our brand at a distance, are all real and provide needed leverage as we and our brand move through the world (#25). Above all, though, there is the beer, and no voice is more important—the ultimate ambassador, the truest envoy, the voice of the beers made by Lagunitas (#26).

Phew, that was hard. I hope it was worth it. The story, for the record, is totally true. Totally.

EPILOGUE

*S*ometimes *an ending is also a beginning. This* is the second edition of this book (the first came out from a tiny publisher, Charles Pinot, in 2012), and so much has happened to Lagunitas in the interim that I wanted to bring the book and you, kind reader, along into our future. Thanks for hanging in with the story all the way to this spot along the highway.

Although the first edition didn't say so, I began this book sitting quietly on the 104-hour warp of the California Zephyr going to Chicago and back for a holiday break with my sister and my three nieces. By the time I wrote the last paragraphs I was waiting in a November rain, broken down in the third verse of a James McMurtry song, along the Will Rogers Turnpike just outside the Oklahoma hamlet of Big Cabin in an old motor home with a guitar, my two dogs, a dozen cases of good beer, and a credit card. I had been moving through time and space toward a then-unseen two-level anterior cervical discectomy-and-fusion followed by more than enough time sitting and sleeping upright while imagining the time when it would all be behind me, practicing good posture, and visualizing spinal synthesis. All in all it would give me more than enough time to finish the numerous rewrites of that first draft.

I was reconnecting with the landscape to which we present our work in the hope that all of this coming and going would reveal a deeper understanding of our place in it all—and along the way maybe even enable me to enjoy a sweet hangover or two—waiting for the monster tow truck to make its way through the central-state rains to my rescue. I was thinking about the future: when I'd get back home, how we'd finance our continued expansion—if we even should keep expanding—how we'd manage to keep the vibe intact as the planet of Lagunitas grew larger. The list of "don't knows" was far longer than the "know for sures."

As I had many times before, I wanted to disappear from this place and reappear, if only for a moment, five years in the future in the middle of the brewery grounds in Petaluma to take even the briefest of peeks at the landscape and see where it was all headed so I could connect my unrealistic expectations with the as-yet-unrealistic future.

Of course, this ain't possible, but the cramping-hard (hard like going to sleep on Christmas eve) alternative was just to wait and see. I wished that there were some mystical conduit I could climb up and actually glimpse our future. For that peek I would pay any price, and I would memorize everything that I could glean from that future scene so that I could come back to my broken-down-two-dog-motorhome-in-the-Oklahoma-rain self and say . . .

THE END OF THE BEGINNING

From 2007 through the present our growth took on an exponential quality from a volumetric standpoint. Even though we'd always grown in a way that hurt, at least a little, the raw numbers were pretty small. If the *percentage* year-over-year growth increases even a little, the actual number of cases under that percentage increase exponentially. But even doubling doesn't amount to much when you're small: 1, 2, 4, 8, 16, 32, 64, 128 . . . But if it continues for very long, the numbers become very large very quickly: 256, 512, 1,024, 2,048, 4,096, 8,192, 16,384, and so on.

Way, way back in 1999, when we moved into our current Petaluma home, I spent a bunch of time considering how much beer we could actually ever hope in our wildest dreams to produce there. It was more of a fantasy trip for me than anything else, but it seemed worth knowing. I had no way of guessing how many fermenters we would be able to put up or what size brew house might ever be possible, but I figured that I could make some pretty good guesses about how many semitrucks we could have enter, stage, unload, load up, and even hang out, given the size of the street entrance and exit and the square footage of driveways and parking lots. That number came out to just about 650,000 barrels. From the point of view of the Jack that we were when we moved into the site at 15,000 barrels, that seemed like a plenty tall beanstalk.

However, when we installed our first eighty-barrel ROLEC brew house in 2009, we began to test the property's ability to allow all of that truck traffic. Then, as we accumulated all of the buildings surrounding the original building, we flew through the 200,000 barrel/year brewing rate and ordered the 250-barrel ROLEC brew house, to the great surprise of the builders. At first they thought I was only kidding them, and they only believed me when I told them we needed it delivered within twelve months.

That was 2010 and, praise the Lord, it was making beer by May 2011. That new brew house hit the ground running too, and within eight months it was running at eight brews per day, five days per week. That meant that it was almost maxed out. We could have fired up the eighty-barrel to run alongside it, but another better idea was hiding in the weeds, waiting to be recognized.

About that time we were looking deep into ways of shortening our lead times for delivery to the various markets in the eastern United States. It's tricky to fill such a long pipeline with product of the correct mix from such a relatively small brewery. Florida might as well have been South Africa, and even NYC was a far-off land during the winter when any number of blizzards or ice storms—or plain old lethargy—might slow the beer by a week or more on the road. The idea arose to rent a warehouse in Chicago and store beer there for shipment so that lead times, as well as two mountain ranges and a desert, would be removed from a delivery. It would cost something to hold that inventory, and we needed a crew there to manage it. In the end we couldn't make it pencil out to a break-even situation, especially in light of our recent revelation that we were only slightly better than breaking even on almost all of the beer we were shipping all the way to New England. So that thought experiment ended with a whimper.

By early 2012 we were starting to think we'd need to get the "old" eighty-barrel brew house going again when, one morning, my wife, Carissa (who handles all of the basic brewery scheduling and ordering of trucks to ship what has been brewed), was complaining to me through the shower door while she was blow-drying her hair about how hard it was to get refrigerated trucks to carry loads east that time of year and that trucks to Florida were the most expensive of all, if they could even be found. She told me the average for most of the eastern US was $1,500 per truck. There are only 1,200 cases on a truck, so that really adds up. I asked her how many trucks we were flinging eastbound each week at that point, and she told me: nine. The eastern United States was our fastest-growing market at that point—just about 100 percent year over year—so that meant that by mid-2013 it might be as many as eighteen trucks each week.

Way back in 2006 when we bought our first bottling line, I sold the idea to a bank by showing that the throughput efficiency of the new bottling line over the old one would make the payment on the line several times over, meaning that the bottling line would make money, not cost it. I applied the same logic upstream to the centrifuge in that it would recover more beer from the fermenter than a plate-and-frame filter could, and so it too would make money, albeit a little less since it was further upstream. And again the same logic was involved in the eighty-barrel brew house. The economics were still pertinent, but the extent to which the brew house covered its own cost was a bit thinner yet, being at the headwaters, as far upstream as you could get. If you want to grow and make more beer, you have to add equipment, but finding a way to pay for it by making it pay for itself is the best way. At least that's how we did it.

All of a sudden, in that early 2012 bathroom conversation, it seemed like that idea was in play again. I couldn't figure out exactly how it applied, but it got me thinking. I got baked in the usual fashion and headed to the brewery taking the long way on the two-lane back roads. At about the halfway point, my itinerant mind was sifting through the clues I'd heard that morning, and all at once the whole thing became as clear as day. Lots of others had come that far more methodically, but this is how it worked for us.

I found a turnout and pulled off the road. I got out a calculator and multiplied eighteen trucks each week by four for a month and then multiplied that by $1,750 per average truck and got about $120,000. That was our cash outlay each month for freight, which is an expense. I looked on my phone and Googled a mortgage calculator so I could enter the $120,000 as our payment to see how much we could borrow. I had to try a whole bunch of mortgage calculators before I found one that would even *let* me put $120,000 in for a monthly payment, but when I did, it told me I could borrow about $24 million! That was plenty enough money to build a whole damn brewery. I knew in an instant that the city would have to be Chicago.

That was news! I was actually sweating a little when I realized what I was seeing on my phone's screen. I drove the rest of the way to the brewery with a totally different buzz than I left my house with. In a sort of transcendental haze, I walked into my CFO's office and grabbed an envelope out of his trash and in about five lines sketched it out. I knew the bank would be willing, since it would allow them to tap the existing cash that was already flowing to trucking companies. On the balance sheet it would be strong, since we would be converting an ongoing expense (freight expense) into an asset (a brewery), and one day we would pay off the brewery, while the freight bill would have gone on forever. It would solve all of the challenges the Chicago ware-house idea had presented. And best of all, from a monthly cash-flow standpoint, we would be building the brewery for free, in that there'd be no change in our cash outflow.

But better than even the best of all was that we'd have an opportunity to make a whole new first-person relationship with a whole new community (as well as my old hometown). I'd left Chicago twenty-five years earlier with my tail between my legs, and suddenly I felt like I'd be able to go back with something to offer. From a personal growth standpoint, it was a very rewarding moment.

Later that morning as I talked with others at the brewery about the idea, a concern arose that people might not think our beer would be the same if it didn't come from the San Francisco area and that I was underestimating the "where" of the brewery. This struck me as a pretty valid concern, but I decided that we should instead be afraid of *not* being able to brew our beer closer to the people who drink it and that our job was to make sure that that was OK with people. In other words, it was imperative that we build a second brewery and that we make a success of it. In the end, beer lovers were excited by the idea, and lots of good things flowed from it all.

There was an interesting complication. If the economics were going to work, then we had to build the new brewery really fast, because it was going to be the capacity that I would have had to add in Petaluma. To make things a little more intense, it quickly became clear that while our West Coast business was growing well, the eastern United States was our most underdeveloped market and so was growing more quickly, meaning that it was urgent (more profitable) to add that capacity closer to the point of consumption.

Every year since the start, in a continuous fashion, we had had to add brewing capacity, fermentation tanks, filtration capacity, warehouse space, water, gas, and electric service—everything. If we were going to build a new brewery in Chicago, then that would actually be our 2014 capacity addition because it would also take about half of the load off of Petaluma, which opened up a lot of future capacity for the western states. In a way, adding one tank in Chicago would be like adding one in Petaluma as well!

But for it to work out, we would need to have the new brewery making beer by early 2014 at the latest, and we didn't even have a building yet.

Then I had to figure out how we were going to accomplish the deed. The enormity of the project was an aspect I ignored. It was too much to swallow, and I only needed to start in order to finish. I Googled "Chicago commercial real estate," and up popped about a million properties, uncorrelated and impossible to sort. Even the question of "how big a building" might take an engineer to solve, except I couldn't wait that long. I was stupid that way. Instead, that same afternoon I just walked around our brewery grounds with a thirty-foot tape measure for about half a day and added up all the buildings and the outdoor tanks and equipment pads, with an extra 15 percent for forklift lanes (since they drive across the parking lots between buildings). I added it all up, and it was 150,000 square feet. If we did it in Petaluma, we could replicate it in Chicago. The space, the tanks, the stuff. Seemed kind of simple.

All of those revelations occurred early one week in February; by the following Friday I had found a realtor on the Internet and he'd sent me twenty potential buildings to do Google Street View drive-bys; and by Monday night I was on a plane to see them. We saw them all on Tuesday and Wednesday and by the end of the first day had potentials but no slam dunk. A building that we could get everything into—fifty-foot-tall fermenters included—would be a great thing, but we hadn't seen anything even close. At the end of the second day the realtor could see we were getting nowhere, and he pulled to the curb and said, "Well, there is one more building, but it's not on the market, and the owner is a pretty particular guy, but I think you should meet him and see it."

The realtor made a call, and twenty minutes later we were walking into a six-acre building: a monstrous, empty, open steel cube with fifty-seven-foot ceilings. It was a building built to fabricate steel components (trusses, I beams, steel plates, etc.), but its destiny clearly was a brewery. As time has passed, I have ceased to believe in coincidences. It was the one building in the entirety of the sprawling city of Chicago that was not only perfect, but also was just sitting, off the market, waiting for our visit.

But the building's most valuable assets were going to be found in the person of its owner.

We walked wide-eyed through the airplane hanger–like building, and then twenty minutes later I was shaking hands with a secret self-made Greek billionaire turned Canadian movie soundstage pioneer turned Chicago movie soundstage pioneer. His name was Nick Mirkopoulos, and he was a seventy-year-old man going on fifty, a pirate king who was as close with Colin Powell as he was with the man who poured concrete for him. He'd founded and sold the largest construction company in Canada and done work all over the world for the CIA and the Pentagon and others whom we mortals will never know about for sure. He had bought the old Ryerson steel buildings in Chicago a few years earlier and immediately began transforming them into the largest movie soundstage complex in North America—a fifty-two-acre collection of four 300,000-square-foot buildings and some other support buildings, with more than a million square feet of high-cube space. Two of the buildings were already turning out films like *Transformers* and a Showtime series called *Boss*, with Kelsey Grammer. Nick was a self-made man in every respect, and in the course of things he had already built two Molson breweries in Canada. So when I met him, he probably knew more about what I was going to do than I did. That would not be the last time he saw my future.

My realtor introduced us, and we—Nick, his CFO, and his Chicago-born-and-bred nephew Alex—sat down around an enormous oak table in a massive cigarette-smoke old-world haze in no-smoking-indoors Chicago. Nick looked at me squarely and asked me what I wanted to do. I described the Petaluma business, our growth, the revelation that had brought me there, our prospects, and the fact that I didn't need any investment from him as landlord, that the business was prepared to do the deed on our own. When I said that last part, he smiled almost imperceptibly and became animated and started talking quickly in a cryptic Greek American dialect that only existed wherever he was. I struggled to keep up, but I got the feeling that I'd made a good impression. In the end, maybe because I didn't ask for anything from him, Nick made everything he had available to me. His generosity was boundless.

It turned out that the realtor had brought a whole bunch of folks by to see the building and meet Nick over the past couple of years, and the usual was that Nick would talk to them for a few minutes and then pat Alex on the shoulder (Alex runs the day-to-day business at the soundstages) and tell him to finish up. That meant that the building was not available to the prospective tenants. Nick was as visceral a person as I'd ever met. Things themselves were real, and making the imagined things in the world real was what he spent his life doing. Airports in developing nations, war reconstruction after third-world coups, breweries in Canada, oil and gas pipelines from here to there, movie soundstages in Chicago—dreams became realities in Nick's hands.

Doing that takes a masterful razor's-edge blend of integrity, raw will, imagination, and work. Eventually we all stood up from the table to walk back to revisit the building together, and as the others left the room first, Nick took me by the arm and said, "You and me, we are a dying breed, we have to look out for each other. You will build your brewery here. I will help you." As I write this now I am crying just a little because Nick died somewhat suddenly late in 2013, and although he did help me build the brewery in ways deep and wide, he did not get to walk through it with me. Over the years I have, in the course of things, collected a lot of father figures who have walked me through waters I might not have navigated so well on my own. People need these things, and businesses need these people too. Lagunitas and I have needed every one of them, for certain.

Initially we had agreed to rent one-half of the building, but as the summer progressed and Petaluma became crazy pressured to brew and ship more beer, we could see our prospects were increasing, so we decided to offer to take the entire building. Nick was very pleased. It meant that he would have less space for additional soundstages, but it also meant that Cinespace (the name of the soundstage business in Toronto as well as Chicago) would have a reliable source of cash flow in the form of our rent for those seasons and sometimes years when the movie business would slow down. We both wanted the same things, and all of our ships were sailing in the same direction.

By late April I had called the astonished Bavarians at ROLEC and ordered yet another 250-barrel brew house, forty more fermenters, eight bottling tanks, another filling line like the one we'd just finished installing in Petaluma, another centrifuge, a boiler, air compressors, and an identical set of everything that we'd just finished upgrading in Petaluma, all for delivery to Chicago within the next fourteen months.

There'd be mountains to move in order to be ready when it all arrived at a loading dock that did not yet exist at 1847 South Washtenaw Avenue in the West Side neighborhoods of Carl Sandburg's "City of the Big Shoulders."

So once everything had been ordered, it was probably time to figure out how to pay for it all. It's important to have one's priorities in order. I mean, why borrow money if you don't have anything to spend it on? We had a meeting previously planned with our bank at their offices in Spokane, Washington, that very March, so, as usual, the stars were aligning in our favor. It was somewhat unprecedented for the bank, in that the CEO and president (two really smart and amazingly soulful guys who had just finished saving the bank from failure in the wake of the 2009 meltdown and in the process made it one of the best capitalized banks on the entire West Coast) had arranged for us to present ourselves, Lagunitas, and its situation directly to the bank's credit committee.

That committee is, in almost every bank, intentionally isolated from the creditor so as to ensure an objective evaluation of the underwriting and credit worthiness of the enterprise itself, apart from the optimism of its management. Although it seems strange to even type these words, it is also true that very few truly capital-intensive businesses like ours ever grow as quickly and strongly as we had been growing; such is the uniqueness of the craft-brewing revolution. Their credit committee had not had any experience with a business case like ours, so the CEO and president wanted the credit committee also to look at the people who were behind the business as an additional consideration. In other words, our credit worthiness was in part based on the strength of our management team, and we were more than ready to present ourselves and our ideas for our future. Our presentation was only intended to show our own back-room strengths along with our planned capital expense projects for Petaluma. On the plane there we had decided to present the Chicago project in an unorthodox way.

We all sat around a huge oak table in big padded chairs in an expansive oak-paneled room on the upper floor of the bank's headquarters, with equally huge windows looking out over a gray March day. Our presentation did not include any work on the Chicago brewery yet, because at that point we had just begun modeling it, really understanding it, and seeing how strong the opportunity was from a business perspective as well as a brand- and beer-lover-connection aspect.

We showed the committee our past, our present, and our future and took their probing questions about risks and vulnerabilities and the strength of our resources to sustain our momentum. It was a fascinating probe of the business and of ourselves, and we represented well. But while we were talking about financing numbers that were already robust, we didn't even mention Chicago, which would be another $20-plus million. After the meeting the bankers planned for us all to go out to a great beer bar in Spokane for a few pints, dinner, and more conversation. As we all loaded out of the bank building, I sidled up next to the CEO and rode with him in his car to the restaurant. As soon as we pulled out of the bank parking lot, I told him that I had something exciting that I wanted to tell him about.

By the time we reached the restaurant, the financing was all but completed. Heading to our table the CEO pulled the chief credit officer aside with me and sat us together, telling him that I had something very interesting to discuss with him. We discussed the logic over brown ales and saisons with pizza, and it was instantly as clear to him as it was to us a few weeks earlier. Every wheel had been set in motion.

Well, almost every wheel. There were still the arduous processes of permitting and building in what might be an indifferent muscle-bound megalopolis. However, I had Nick Mirkopoulos in my corner. "You will build your brewery. I will help you," he had said. So said, so done. Nick readily partnered me with his state legislative consultant (a nice term for lobbyist), his own well-resourced attorney in a very tall building downtown looking down on city hall, his own handpicked design-build team on-site at the Cinespace Studios, his own on-site construction teams—everything that there was to be shared was shared. Within a few weeks I'd met with the governor of Illinois (never did meet Arnold), the mayor's office, our neighborhood's alderman, important individuals in the building departments, and beyond.

Most good companies would take a year just to vet the idea, and only then would there be site-selection teams and lawyers pursuing government grants, engineering studies and utility and wastewater investigations, and consumer research and logistics studies commissioned. But for me, once you can see through to the essential logic of a decision, the rest is mere detail and execution. For the record, a month later I was driving east on Highway 80 through Fairfield, California, and as I drove past the three-million-barrel ABI brewery there, I realized that they were already doing it, that was how it was supposed to work, and that I'd reinvented a very well-worn wheel. I was still jazzed, though.

GOVERNMENT INCENTIVES & THE HORSE YOU RODE IN ON

Early on in the two days we spent looking for a building, the realtor, a very experienced and savvy guy, advised me to contact the City of Chicago's outreach program because there were significant financial incentives that I could get from the city, but it would be important not to sign a lease before the city proposed the incentive money. If I did sign a lease, the city could not make the "but for this incentive" finding to show that if it had not offered the incentive, I might have located the brewery in an adjacent town or in Indiana or Wisconsin. I had no intention of being anywhere but inside the Chicago city limits. I want to put the city where the beer is brewed on the label, and the Chicago brewery would be shipping beer to London and Edinburgh and beyond. I don't think any Glaswegians have any idea where Bedford Park or Cicero are located. Chicago is one of the capitals of the world.

All at once, the great pretense was beginning. In order to "get," I would have to lie a little bit, manipulate, assume positions not my own, and be less than genuine. All of that seemed to be "high business" thinking, and all at once, on the second day, I jettisoned the idea. In any case, I knew that I didn't need the money from the city. Conventional wisdom called me a fool for "leaving money on the table."

Everybody told me, "This is how the game is played." The more I heard why it was such a good idea, the more turned off I became to the whole notion of gamesmanship as business. In business there are games to be played and games that must be won, but asking a city to fork over real-estate tax receipts under false (even if conventional) pretenses just seemed wrong. Instantly, though, in aligning what I wanted with what I needed, I found some very unusual high ground to stand on.

The government incentive money would be drawn from real-estate taxes in the same area in which the brewery would be built. It is a neighborhood with social problems, a little crime, some real poverty, and lots of potholes. Why would I want to siphon off that money? But it is conventional; it is even a sort of business "wisdom" to demand it. We didn't need it, I wouldn't want anyone knowing that I'd accepted it, and even as I sat in the car with the realtor and scrubbed the idea off and declined even the pursuit of the subsidy, I felt better about myself. An office on the nose of a fast train is a difficult environment in which to make "thoughtful" decisions, and more times than not, what just feels right is the best compass to trust.

In the subsequent meetings with very senior city and state officials I always took the opportunity to say that we were not pursuing grants or tax incentives of any kind and that Lagunitas didn't need any incentive to be in Chicago, that the city itself was enough of an attractor and we were going to be proud to say that we never even considered any other town. Saying that aloud in meetings with city staff always elicited a raised eyebrow or two combined with an easy smile that seemed to say, *Well, that's why I'm here too!* It's always good when you want what your partners also want.

But here's a larger thing to think about. I believe that Lagunitas is the sort of place that it is because of the things that I and the others who lead the company think are good and worthwhile. We highlight those things in our own work and in what we do and say, and so they have become the texture of the company. The same is completely true of the larger world. The things we engage with become emphasized and grow in importance while the things we eschew are marginalized and recede. I wonder if you, kind reader, would want for the real-estate taxes collected in your area to be given to me so that I could build a brewery. Why should I feel entitled to your tax money? Because I'm bringing jobs? Is that a win-win? Maybe. Oh, I remember, it was the "but for" finding, meaning that if the city didn't fork over that real-estate tax money, I'd have put the brewery in the next town over, because they *would* offer me money. This was not something that I wanted to engage with.

For some businesses these things can actually be the difference between being *able* to do a project or not being able. Those are the deserving. That wasn't the case for Lagunitas. So we demurred. It's worth thinking about the idea that we create the world around us by the decisions that we make, large and small. Conventional wisdom can be the enemy of a better community.

THE SECOND BREWERY AS THE END OF OUR START-UP PERIOD

The commissioning of the second brewery in Chicago was, in the final accounting, far more for us than just another location of additional capacity. It signaled the end of our time as a start-up business. Most people think of the start-up phase as the time a business was located in someone's parents' garage, but in a capital-intensive consumer product that phase can stretch out for a decade or more before you really know if you've created a long-term proposition. We were two decades into it before we had the confidence to put a second leg on our pogo stick.

The second leg is important for a whole host of reasons. First, it provides real redundancy. In Petaluma we are always at the mercy of our one bottling line, our one brew house, our one filtration rig, our one keg line, etc. Since most of us small brewers are brewing close to whatever capacity we can afford, any failure of a pump seal or a filler valve stops the entire train. Those shutdowns are routine things: stuff wears out, and sometimes it fails. But larger failures can occur.

For instance, California is currently (2014) in the midst of the most severe drought since 1897. Will it go on for two years? Maybe ten years? Even if water is still available, when supplies are stressed, metals and other problematic constituents rise, and brewing quality goes downhill very quickly. How about an 8.0 earthquake? The brewery is engineered to that standard of toughness, but there are still power requirements and other utilities, not to mention roads and bridges. Natural disasters are long shots, but if a brewery grows large, there is a large payroll to meet and debt service to answer to all the same.

Beyond that, there is the maturing of the operations. When we are all across the parking lot from each other, it's easy to holler to get an answer. But the overnight brewer usually has to make guesses while the front office is asleep. Operating two plants twenty-five hundred miles apart in a manner that is as seamless as if they were across the street from each other requires seamless systems and processes where everything we do every day is integrated and extremely well understood. I think of this as a "curing" process, in which we go from being a bit spongy to robust, reliable, and long-term in our approach. It is the end of the beginning and the beginning of something far deeper.

THE CURRENT, CURRENT PLANET OF LAGUNITAS

The first paragraph of this book says plainly that "This is a memoir of the starting of a business." It was not meant to be a personal story, but this last part is. The whole story frames a real life, because, like some, I do have a wife and parents and siblings and furniture and in-laws and no kids. The no-kids part made some of the high-wire act more doable because what I was risking wouldn't have had an impact on anyone besides my wife and me, and we're grown-ups and could live with the outcomes. But it was still messy, with a capital *M*.

We've been through enough to have confidence in ourselves by now. Many of Lagunitas's 1993 peers did go quietly into the night during the mid and late 1990s. Many of the ones who survived were correctly capitalized from an early age, and so when the poop hit the blades, they were able to rejigger their business strategy and come out the other end looking like the shiny, happy people they are. We weren't like that. But we survived just the same. As a Confederate general once ironically declared, "We can't lose, because we'll never give up." I was working without a net, not because I thought it was nobler or more honest, but because I didn't know any better. Everything comes from somewhere, and I came from the basement of business skills and a certain sort of poverty of the pocket. Having done it the way I did provided a very intense experience but not a better one.

For the first twelve years I was never the highest-paid employee, and as the overlap of my previous business faded away, my wife and I enjoyed a nice enough lifestyle lived on a precipice. It was OK, but it was also populated with bill collectors, tax collectors, genuine repo men, and luck in the form of uniformly good health. On more than one occasion my wife pointed out to me that to cover our household expenses we were relying on personal tax refunds resulting from business losses at the brewery. That's creepy. Lotsa folks do it, but it is unhealthy in every way imaginable.

However, you do get the chance to learn how the world really works, which is a priceless education. In particular you learn how valuable a reputation can be and that not all equivalent transactions are treated equally. That sometimes people are willing to steal from you if you are too trusting. You learn that some friendships are very real, and that's a great thing.

You also start to learn things that you wish you didn't know. Some of the harder things you learn are about yourself, while other lessons reveal the lesser inclinations and projected fears of people you care about or thought you knew well—all occurring in the shadow of the silhouette of a force that does not care if you succeed or not and wants its share of your work even if it crushes you in the process. You learn that parts of government can be sneaky and that it dislikes the habits of its adult citizens. I'm not just talking about weed here, but weed and beer itself and employment taxes, property taxes, excise taxes (paid up front just like real drug money), a thousand miscellaneous fees and tolls that all conspire to put a straw deep down into the gut of your start-up enterprise to draw off its juices in the same way that a spider digests its living prey.

I'm a notch older than fifty, and after all the heavy lifting and the all-or-nothing moments, I sometimes feel on the far side of the same. I still love the work of inhabiting the Lagunitas brand, being the hand inside the ventriloquist's puppet, the ghost in the machine, but the other less visible and all-important back-room aspects of the business have become less attractive to me. They say you always blunt the tool you work with. In a lot of ways I'm ready to forget everything I have learned, join Siddhartha on the oxen road, and return to the world and just drink good beer with it all. The idea of being a fast-growing brewery or just to be well loved by the thousand faceless judges at the beer-rating websites sometimes weighs heavily.

Our job now is to keep it all real and real fun as we become a real business among businesses and not to allow those burdens to overwhelm the enviable thing that we all actually do for a living: make a tasty adult beverage. Thank you for the last twenty years of learning and growing in every way, and I hope that we can live up to the hopes of future beer lovers in the United States—and beyond that to the old worlds that lie to the east and west, north and south. Cheers, brothers and sisters!

INDEX